FIGHT
FOR THE
FAMILY

JILL BRISCOE

FIGHT FOR THE FAMILY

Lamplighter Books Grand Rapids, Michigan
Zondervan Publishing House

FIGHT FOR THE FAMILY

Copyright © 1981 by The Zondervan Corporation
Grand Rapids, Michigan

Lamplighter Books are published by Zondervan
Publishing House, 1415 Lake Drive, S.E.,
Grand Rapids, Michigan 49506

Library of Congress Cataloging in Publication Data

Briscoe, Jill.
Fight for the family.

1. Family–Moral religious aspects. 2. Bible.
O.T. Nehemiah–Criticism, interpretation, etc.
I. Title.
HQ734.B8158   306.8   81-16068
ISBN 0-310-21841-1   AACR2

Edited by Linda DeVries and Judith E. Markham

85 86 87 88 — 10 9 8 7 6 5

To Stuart, David, Judy, and Peter

For whom I am profoundly grateful,
    by whom I am most marvelously loved,
and to whom I owe a debt of thankfulness
    I shall never be able to repay.
Thank you anyway—
    for the solid, blessed base of my belonging
        that you have made for me.
For my coming home to tight, tired touches of
    your tenderness that told me you
        missed me but you managed.
    For ready responses and
        kept kisses—just for me.
For all the harnessed humor
    reigned in with cautious care
That hurried me along into the sweet and
    certain sureness of my place in
        your affections.
Thank you for the little letters—
            naughty notes—
        protracted phone bills,
    reminding me in terms of cold, crass cash
        of shared concerns as well as all the
            relevant irrelevancies,
        most necessary news to me
            of mourned,
                missed
                    moments we couldn't spend together!
Yes, thank you for letting me live in the
    matrix of that mother-wife
        hole in your hearts.
And this because of Him who made our
    moments and counted out our days,
this God of love—
    who gifted us all with the rare reality of
        one of redemption's richest rewards—
            a regenerate family!

About the Worksheets

The Worksheets at the end of each chapter have been designed to encourage discussion and application of the material. They can be used in Sunday school, home Bible studies, or adapted for family devotions.

Contents

Foreword by Cliff Barrows

A popular commercial says, "I'd rather fight than switch." Unfortunately, as far as the family is concerned, the ever-growing accepted concept is "I'd rather switch than fight."

Jill Briscoe does not share that view, and it seems that she's in mighty good company. She uses the story of Nehemiah and his burden for the remnant of Israel who remained in Jerusalem during the captivity as an analogy to apply spiritual principles in rebuilding the walls of the family.

Jill's extraordinary grasp of spiritual truth and its practical application to everyday living will keep this book off the shelf and in front of you in exciting and helpful reading. Personal illustrations provide some of the most effective windows to truth, and Jill doesn't hesitate to share these with you from her own family experiences. Having known Stuart and Jill Briscoe for many years . . . being in their home . . . and observing the growth and development of their children David, Judy, and Peter, I've witnessed firsthand their commitment to the family and to the principles that Jill presents in these pages. This is not a collection of clever clichés or pious platitudes that have little or no relevance to today's world. On the contrary, I believe you will find, as I have, that these fresh insights into scriptural truth are personal, practical, and very helpful.

There are unbelievable forces at work today in our society, forces that are committed to the destruction of the Christian concept of the family. It is crumbling all around us, and some of the most vulnerable are those who a few years ago would have said, "It won't and can't happen to me." What can we do about it? Is the family worth fighting for? Is there hope for the "remnant" who are not willing to throw in the towel and call it quits? Jill believes there is, and I do too. We CAN rebuild the walls. We CAN stand up and "fight for the family." This much-needed book tells us why and shows us how!

Introduction

The Christian concept of the family is under incredible attack in the age in which we live. The walls have fallen down, and all that remains of many homes—even those built on Christian foundations—are heaps of rubble. Today, like the remnant of Israel left behind in Jerusalem, only a small number of God's people who care about God's name appear to be left to do something with the heap! And as soon as anyone bends down to lift the first brick, we can be sure the opposition will appear. Nehemiah certainly found it to be so. But listen to his words of encouragement and challenge, and "strengthen [your] hands" for this good work:

> Therefore I stationed some of the people behind the lowest points of the wall at the exposed places, posting them by families, with their swords, spears and bows. After I looked things over, I stood up and said to the nobles, the officials and the rest of the people, "Don't be afraid of them. Remember the LORD, who is great and awesome, and fight for your brothers, your sons and your daughters, your wives and your homes" (Neh. 4:13-14).

In other words, *fight for the family!*

THE BURDEN

1

The Wall Is Fallen Down

Count if you can the homes that lie in ruins, the children who cry for their fathers, the wives who gaze in terror around the corner of tomorrow wondering how they will ever cope alone to face the foe. Like the ancient city of Jerusalem, the walls have fallen down around our families, and it is time for those who care to "rise up and build"!

Listen to the words of Nehemiah, son of Hacaliah:

> In the month of Kislev in the twentieth year, while I was in the citadel of Susa, Hanani, one of my brothers, came from Judah with some other men, and I questioned them about the Jewish remnant that survived the exile, and also about Jerusalem. They said to me, "Those who survived the exile and are back in the province are in great trouble and disgrace. The wall of Jerusalem is broken down, and its gates have been burned with fire" (Neh. 1:1-3).

Nehemiah was engaged in a slightly dangerous occupation, to say the least. He was the king's cupbearer (1:11), a job that meant tasting his majesty's brew to find out whether or not it had been poisoned. If Nehemiah dropped dead, everyone would know that it had been! He was also expected to smile happily throughout this extremely hazardous duty, the thinking apparently being that even a slave could not fail to be charmed in the service of the king.

After receiving the bad news about the plight of the families left in Jerusalem, Nehemiah "sat down and wept. For some days [he] mourned and fasted and prayed before the God of heaven" (1:4).

Who Will Fight?

In those days a city without walls was not the sort of real estate people were looking for; without adequate protection a town was vulnerable to anyone who wanted to march in and carry off a wife, rape a maiden, or steal and plunder people's possessions. It was obvious to Nehemiah that the city must be rebuilt, beginning with the walls. God's family was in jeopardy and God's name was at stake. "Those who survived the exile," Nehemiah was told, "are . . . in great trouble and disgrace" (1:3). God's reputation was on the line, for it was His city that lay wasted, His gates that were burned, His laws that had been forsaken, and His promises that had been ignored. Someone needed to *fight for the family*.

One of the most frightening aspects of the disintegration of the family in our day and age has been the way God's people have begun to be part of the problem rather than part of the solution. *The statistics have come to church.* Maybe last Sunday you even sat next to a new statistic and shared your hymnbook with him or her. Many of us have acclimatized too quickly to the chill wind of changing values and have simply buttoned up our topcoats of indifference to prevent the icy blast from touching our hearts. My question is this: When is someone going to get angry enough to do what Nehemiah did—fight for the family? As we see the walls falling down around us, we certainly should mourn this carnage of human relationships. But there is another factor that ought to move us to action: God's reputation is at stake. As believers divorce, children rebel, and the family disintegrates, God's good name is brought into disrepute.

Faith As a Weapon

Nehemiah must have felt deep frustration when he heard the bad news brought to him by his brother, and I can see him wondering desperately what he, a mere slave, could do. He knew he wasn't free to leave his place of "employment" and volunteer for foreign service. He couldn't even show his deep distress in public, for to do so would mean certain death. But prayer and care result in "Dare"; and Nehemiah, albeit with a trembling heart, decided to trust the God of the miraculous to do the ridiculous and so work in the king's life that he would grant his petition—however wild it appeared to be. Believe it or not, Nehemiah decided to ask for a working vacation back home—for an unspecified number of months! No wonder we read that he was "very much afraid" as he handed the king his wine and was interrogated concerning his fallen countenance.

"'Why does your face look so sad when you are not ill?'" the king asked him. "'This can be nothing but sadness of heart'" (2:2). Then said Nehemiah, "I was very much afraid, *but. . . .*" The "buts" of the Bible are often beautiful bridges used to cross from the depths of despair to the mountains of hope. In this instance, Nehemiah's "but" was the bridge from the fear of his earthly monarch to faith in his heavenly King! "But I said to the king, 'May the king live forever! Why should my face not look sad when the city where my fathers are buried lies in ruins, and its gates have been destroyed by fire?'" Then the king asked Nehemiah, "'What is it you want?'" (2:3-4). Oh, joy! Who is more than conqueror now? The slave free in his heart because he is slave to his God!

The Bible tells us that at this point Nehemiah prayed to the God of heaven. You bet he did! Wouldn't you have prayed harder and faster than you ever had in your whole life? Aren't you challenged by Nehemiah's daring spirit, regardless of the consequences to himself, and by his determination to think big and pray for dreams mixed with faith to turn into glorious realities? God is still God and able to bring glory to Himself out of any situation.

Nehemiah received his vacation—a free trip home, letters of safe conduct for his journey, timber for the gates of Jerusalem and the house that he would occupy, and even army officers and cavalry to protect him (2:7-9)! The powerful, earthly monarch proceeded to inquire humbly of God's slave, "How long will your journey take, and when will you be back?" (2:6).

When will you be back indeed! Hear Nehemiah's reply: "So I set a time"! said Nehemiah. "I" set a time! We must believe it really happened, for history tells us it was so. We must applaud the audacity of faith! Is not our God a marvelous Hearer of prayer and Worker of miracles? History is surely "His story," and He tells it as He wills. You see, God's purposes were involved, and He was committed to working out His eternal designs despite the crumbling walls of His city, the bands of rebels brandishing their little dust fists in His face, and one of His favorite children apparently confined to servitude. As Nehemiah explains it, "*Because* the gracious hand of my God was upon me, the king granted my requests" (2:8). Nehemiah believed, as the Scriptures say, that "the king's heart is in the hand of the LORD; he directs it like a watercourse wherever he pleases" (Prov. 21:1). And so Nehemiah went to Jerusalem.

Where to Begin

At this point I can imagine that many of you are saying to yourselves, "Well, that's nice, but Nehemiah was Nehemiah, and I am just little old me!" Perhaps you've looked around and seen the walls crumbling around the family. You have kept up with the reports through the media and consider yourself conversant with the facts. You can even quote learned gentlemen like Nathan Ackerman, who has said pessimistically:

I am a psychiatrist who has devoted a lifetime to studying emotional problems of family living. I have pioneered in the field of family therapy. From where I sit the picture of marriage and family in present day society is a gloomy one. Family life seems to be cracking at the seams and an *effective mortar is nowhere available.* [1]

As you have received news of people's relationships in danger or in trouble, I'm sure you must have chafed and fretted, not knowing what you could do to change the situation. There may have been a rape, a bereavement, or a divorce. In fact, the walls have fallen down! Like Nehemiah, you may live too far away to help, or you may feel the situation is so bad that all is lost and in ruins. You probably don't think of yourself as some great crusading Nehemiah anyway. Even if you did, you believe the people involved have become too embittered to listen to you. But don't you think Nehemiah felt like that?

There may be another problem. If you are a Christian and the walls have fallen down around your own marriage, it may be that you cannot envisage ever holding your head up high again, let alone rummaging among the rubbish for a brick. As you sit in the dust of your disintegrated relationship, a slave of your circumstances, fettered into immobility, you simply ask to be left alone to lick your wounds and relive the "invasion" of your land and personal property over and over again. But don't you think Nehemiah felt like that?

Listen as he prays to the Lord God about the situation and admits his *own* culpability: "I confess the sins we Israelites, *including myself and my father's house,* have committed against you. We have acted very wickedly toward you. We have not obeyed the commands, decrees and laws you gave your servant Moses" (Neh. 1:6-7). From his own personal captivity Nehemiah acknowledged his own iniquity and his family's failures. He knew that this great disaster was a result of their rebellion against God. *But that was where he started—not finished.* That was the beginning, not the end.

Nehemiah was not going home to tell his people he would build the wall *for* them; rather, he would help them begin to build it themselves. He knew the only way this could be accomplished was by the mobilization and involvement of every man, woman, and child in the land. There needed to be something for every member of the family to do. He would encourage everyone to build up the wall in front of their own house (see 3:23). And that is how it has to be for us as well. We must start where we are with what we have. If the walls are to be rebuilt, everyone has to help, from the youngest to the oldest, from the richest to the poorest. Whatever has happened to us in the past must not be allowed to paralyze our present or flaw our future—failure is never final if God is on our side.

A friend of mine whose husband had left her after many years of marriage was sitting among the rubbish contemplating ending it all. How useless she felt. How ashamed. What a failure she believed herself to be. Sharing her despair with another Christian, she received the following advice: "If you take your life, you will have to face Jesus Christ; and when you face Him, you will have to say, 'You weren't enough.'" She decided that night she would rather stay and face the mess than face the Master and say, "You weren't enough." In other words, she picked up a brick. She decided to stay and start to rebuild instead of disintegrating and becoming part of the rubble around her.

Surveying the Walls: Assessing the Damage

Once safely back in Jerusalem, Nehemiah found himself some four-legged transport and set out alone and at night to survey the damage. He found the situation every bit as bad as he had feared. "So I went up the valley by night, examining the wall," he writes (2:15). In some places the destruction was so bad that there was not enough room for his mount to get through (2:14). This did not discourage Nehemiah. In fact, during his practical and realistic look at the situation, God put some things "in [his] heart to do" (2:12).

If we will walk around our marriage as openly as Nehemiah walked around the walls of Jerusalem, surveying the damage, assessing the breaches, and examining the cracks, we can be sure our God will put some things in *our* hearts *to do* as well! The problem comes when we will not do them, or, worse still, refuse to even examine our marriage because we are scared of what we may find. It's easier to bury our heads in the sand and play ostrich, insisting, "It will never happen to us!" Never say never!

Take a trip with God around your relationships and ask Him to help you to see things as He sees them. What He tells us to do about our situation will undoubtedly be quite different from the things He told Nehemiah to do about his, but the principles will be the same.

Motivation

Returning to the people the next day, Nehemiah spoke first to the officials, priests, and nobles. (2:16-17), believing that the leadership had to be aroused from their lethargy. He knew the example of the nobles was very important, for if leaders won't lead, the flock won't follow. "Let us rebuild the wall of Jerusalem," Nehemiah exhorted them as they stood together among the ruins (2:17). "Let us start!" the majority of men responded enthusiastically (2:18).

There were, however, some among the nobles who would not "put their shoulders to the work" (3:5). Cocking their noble noses in the air, they disdained the whole venture. We don't know why those particular men refused to help. Maybe their homes were complete and their families doing fine; maybe that is why they couldn't get too excited about getting their hands dirty. If this was indeed the case, they were extremely selfish and shortsighted. To live in a nice house with inadequate defenses was an open invitation to the enemy.

History has shown that society is strong only when the marriage bond is held in honor. We simply cannot afford to sit tight and do nothing because "our" home is intact. Whether you are a *Nehemiah,* a *noble,* or a *nobody,* each and every one must rise up and build, that "we will no longer be in disgrace" (2:17).

Models

As we begin to get busy outside our own front doors, we will discover we are not alone. We'll notice the family who is busy building right there next to us. What a relief to realize that *they* have to work on the walls as well! Down through the years others have allowed us to observe them as they learned to lay a firm foundation for their marriage. Because of this we have tried to have the courage, confidence, and honesty to let others watch us as well. We all need models of growth and learning—but I hasten to add, *not* models of perfection!

I remember one particular couple who were an immense encouragement to Stuart and me. Their marriage was solid, and the atmosphere of their home gave us a comfortable sense of security. They were two people whose "no option out" commitment had stood the test of time. Opening their hearts and home to young couples, they shared their love—letting us watch it all. I remember looking at the little plaque on our door that said GUEST ROOM and thinking that it should have read OBSERVATION POST, for that is really how we felt about our visits. We found ourselves imbibing attitudes and influences into our own relationships. We couldn't help but overhear the honest sharing of the truth about things even when a lie would have been so much easier to tell; and we noted their saving sense of humor as they refused to take themselves too seriously. Most of all, we found ourselves wanting to emulate their determination to "make it work" at all costs, because they loved the Lord and honored His name more than they honored their own!

I didn't realize how fully I had absorbed their example until recently. Stuart had just come home from work. Taking off his coat, he asked me, "Did you call Mrs. Jones as I asked you to?" I had not! Caught off guard and not wanting him to know about my carelessness, I quickly answered, "Yes!" As soon as it was out, my fertile and deceptive mind went to work, plotting a manipulation of my husband's movements out of the kitchen and upstairs to his study so that I could call Mrs. Jones! Safely out of sight, I scurried into the living room to deliver the important message to the woman in question. She wasn't home!

Standing in the middle of the kitchen, I realized I had told Stuart a lie! After a decade of missionary work, time spent in the pastorate, and years of marriage—yes, after all that practice time—I had lied to my husband! That is not to say there had not been other lies over the years. Some had been dealt with and some, alas, had not; but today was today, and all that I had, and I needed to decide what to do.

Appearing at the top of the stairs, Stuart inquired again, "Jill, *did* you call Mrs. Jones?"

"Yes," I answered brightly.

My husband retired to his desk and a pile of correspondence. I knew that Mrs. Jones would soon be home, so Stuart need never know about my silly deception. Surely it wouldn't matter if I just took care of it and continued on my merry way. But I knew better than that. It did matter. It mattered very much.

It killed me to do it, but after practically crawling up the stairs, I poked my head around the corner of the study and said, "Stuart, I *didn't* call Mrs. Jones!"

My husband looked at me and simply said, "I know!"

We smiled at each other, and I retreated downstairs to make the call. I share this with you not because it makes me feel good to tell you I told a lie, and not because I'm smug about owning up to it, but simply because I want you to know that every Christian couple must learn the building trade. I tell you this because I want you to see me outside my own front door building up the wall.

One of the foundation stones of a good marriage is honesty —an attempt to always tell each other the truth. Lying about little things can soon grow into deceptions about big things, and this makes a definite crack in the wall! There is no such thing as a couple who does it all right, but there are couples who refuse to allow it to go all wrong!

"You mean you and Stuart squabble?" asked a friend incredulously as I recounted a difference of opinion we had had.

"Sometimes," I replied.

"You mean you don't agree on everything?" asked another.

"Of course not," I answered again, recalling Ruth Graham's succinct statement when asked the same question: "If Billy and I agreed on everything, one of us would be unnecessary!"

I thought of the time we had been staying in the OBSERVATION POST and our friends had butted heads about some irritating habit the wife had. Glaring at her husband over the kitchen sink, she had come out with a quick flash of grim humor. "Harry," she had said ominously, "you had all the world to choose from, and you chose me—now be satisfied!" She was right. He had had all the world to choose from and had freely chosen her as his life partner, for better or for worse—there was no argument about that! It was the "now be satisfied" bit that needed thinking about!

God Is on Our Side

If I call myself a Christian, I need to believe that there is "no option out" of my marriage. If I would seek to honor His name, then I have to "work out" in my family what God has been "working into my heart." God is on our side, you see; marriage is *His* idea, and therefore *He* stands behind it. Because that is the case, He has promised to make available to us the power we will need to "now be satisfied!" He will show us how to adapt, accept each other, and work on our differences together.

I believe a Christian home should be like a womb, giving the growing embryo of our marriage a place to safely develop, a space to move and stretch, to cry and struggle until finally our relationship is fully developed and mature. By the same token, I believe a divorce is like an abortion—a thing that never should be, an end instead of a beginning, a severing of life. God hates divorce (Mal. 2:16), although He makes it a legal possibility for those who refuse to allow Him to deal with the obdurate hardness of their hearts. Thus, we have to face the facts. Marriages *have* fallen apart, but life *must* go on. So we have to clear up the mess the best we can and, God helping us, rise up and rebuild.

Notes

1Nathan Ackerman, *Psychodynamics of Family Life* (New York: Basic Books, 1958).

Worksheet

A. *Review*
1. Read Nehemiah 1-2; 4:14.
   a. Share your feelings about the situation of the family in today's society. Do you see evidence that the walls are broken down, that the statistics have come to church?
   b. What legitimate excuses did Nehemiah have *not* to get involved?
   c. What are the excuses that *we* give? (Have each member of the group think of one.)
2. Read Ephesians 6:10-17.
   a. Whom are we fighting?
   b. What commands must we obey (vv. 10-11, 14)? List them.
   c. What promises can we claim (v. 16)?
   d. What armor must we use? Write a sentence about or discuss how each piece of armor will shield, reinforce, and protect us as we fight for our families. (E.g.: Truth will give us a measuring stick to evaluate present value systems with our children [v. 14].)
3. Review the experience of Elisha's servant from 2 Kings 6:15-17. What does this story "say" to you? Apply the things you learn from this passage to your family situation. (E.g.: There are unseen forces *on my side* if I am trying to fight for my family.)
4. Why do *all* God's people need to help?
   Do you see yourself as a Nehemiah, a noble, or a nobody? Why?
5. Why do we need models? What sort of models do we need? Has there been one helpful "brick" that someone has handed you through the years to "firm up the walls"? Have each person share briefly.

B. *Reflect*
What has God impressed upon you from the lesson? Think about it; then talk to Him about it in prayer (silently or corporately).

C. *Reinforce*
If you are married:
1. Decide there is "no option out" for you as a believer and ask God to begin to help you to "now be satisfied."
2. Before the next lesson, walk around your family relationships with God and survey the damage.
3. Reach out and pick up a brick!

THE BOUNDARIES

2

The Battle for
the Boundaries

When Sanballat heard that we were rebuilding the wall, he became angry and was greatly incensed. He ridiculed the Jews, and in the presence of his associates and the army of Samaria, he said, "What are those feeble Jews doing? Will they restore their wall? Will they offer sacrifices? Will they finish in a day? Can they bring the stones back to life from those heaps of rubble—burned as they are?" Tobiah the Ammonite, who was at his side, said, "What they are building—if even a fox climbed up on it, he would break down their wall of stones!" (Neh. 4:1-3).

Meanwhile, the people in Judah said, "The strength of the laborers is giving out, and there is so much rubble that we cannot rebuild the wall" (4:10).

In his inaugural speech a former president expressed the sentiment that when his term in office had ended, he hoped people would be able to say that he had strengthened the American family. A few years later, government surveys showed a weakening of the family structure rather than a strengthening, and the walls continue to crumble at an alarming rate today.

Who Sets the Limits?

Perhaps we need to begin by asking ourselves some questions concerning these walls or boundaries that we keep talking about. Who sets the limits for the relationships within the family anyway? The Bible says God has set the bounds and has given us His good reasons for living within them. After all, the institution of marriage is God's good idea. Someone may quip, "Who wants to live in an institution?" as they conjure up pictures of grim, blackened buildings housing mental patients or the worn aged wearing thin as paper in antiseptic wards. That is not quite what is meant by the word institution, for the real meaning is, "an arrangement of rules for the common good." God, then, has set up the institution of marriage for the benefit, not the bane, of us all!

In the beginning God gave the insects, birds, fish, and animals a family. He said that this arrangement was "very good." However, when God saw Adam without a family, He decided that wasn't very good. He redressed the situation by giving him Eve. Adam was living in Paradise at the time, but apparently Paradise wasn't enough. It took a family to make the difference.

Psalm 68:6 confirms that it is God who sets the solitary in families, and that little word "in" presupposes boundaries. If we believe marriage was conceived in the mind of God and fashioned in the heart of God, then we will not have too much trouble believing that the walls He places around our families have been put there to protect us: to keep trouble out and love in—to be, in fact, boundaries of blessing! Family relationships lived out within God's clearly drawn lines result in solid strength and security. Remember, history teaches us that society is strong only when the marriage bond is held in honor.

"The city [of Jerusalem] was large and spacious, but there were few people in it, and the houses had not yet been rebuilt" (7:4). Seeing this, Nehemiah invited some of the families who had been living "outside" the walls to come and live "inside" them. There was no attempt to force them to comply—just an invitation and a reminder that there was much room to move, grow, and develop within the comparative security of the city walls.

When Nehemiah gave that invitation, the boundaries were quite clearly defined; even though they lay in ruins, that there was no way anyone could say that they didn't know the difference between living within the walls and living without them! But today things are different. The ruined boundaries have been buried under so much rubble that confusion lies within the minds of many. "What does a real marriage consist of anyway?" inquire puzzled, mixed-up teen-agers. "Are you telling us," they ask, "that two people living in hatred and hostility within the walls of their legal contract—proud possessors of a marriage certificate—are any more married than two lovers who genuinely care for each other yet who do not possess that magic piece of paper?" Our children are listening to those free spirits who, eager to cast off all restraint, are arguing that life outside the walls "with love" will surely please a loving God much more than life within the walls without it!

Opinion-Makers

One of the problems we are facing concerns the people who are answering these questions for our youngsters. If child asks child, or teen seeks counsel from teen, or hurt and rejected adult inquires from hurt and rejected adult, the danger is that the response may be given only from the basis of their personal experience—colored by circumstance.

A War of Words

When Nehemiah arrived in Jerusalem, he was met by a war of words and found himself facing a well-organized opposition party headed up by three learned gentlemen, Sanballat, Tobiah, and Geshem, whose main intent was to hinder his work. These were men who had "no share in Jerusalem or any claim or historic right to it" (2:20). They were people whose roots were in other cultures and who had rejected the ways and authority of Nehemiah's God. Moreover, they were "very much disturbed that someone had come to promote the welfare of the Israelites" (2:10). They began to use their considerable prestige and power to intimidate the people, for in their opinion it was ludicrous to even consider reestablishing the boundaries of the city. "Sanballat the Horonite, Tobiah the Ammonite official and Geshem the Arab . . . mocked and ridiculed us. 'What is this you are doing?' they asked. 'Are you rebelling against the king?'" (2:19).

Sanballat, Tobiah, and Geshem are with us today. We meet them every time we pick up a newspaper, peruse a periodical, or switch on the TV. They are symbolic of our modern mind molders who gather new thoughts, formulate opinions, and then project them into the minds of the masses through the media. They appear to have such a thorough grasp of the facts, such a vast accumulation of knowledge. They are so well-informed! They seem to be people we would listen to!

But the Bible says that the wisdom of this world is foolishness compared with God's wisdom (1 Cor. 1:20-25), and that is why I dare to suggest that many of the opinion makers' opinions are mere nonsense. It doesn't make any sense at all to leave God's opinions out of the reckoning, and yet that is what the modern Sanballats, Tobiahs, and Geshems are doing today. They are "always learning but never able to acknowledge the truth" (2 Tim. 3:7).

When an "expert" or "an authority in the field" writes a couple of books entitled *Healthy Adultery* and *Healthy Divorce*, people feel they have to give his or her thesis some consideration. There is real impact when a person as intelligent as the late Dr. Margaret Mead, the anthropologist, suggests that we *must* find a substitute for the American family! But human knowledge that is not illuminated by divine wisdom is not necessarily the truth. Humanism, the essence of which is attributing deity to humanity, teaches that truth is to be found only on the horizontal level and that our social-behavioral patterns can be decided by fallible people, who then proceed to teach us their beliefs about what is right and wrong in an infallible vein.

David Garth, political media consultant who each day enjoys a multi-media feed, told a magazine interviewer that his office clips thirty newspapers, keeps three TV sets on at once, and plays all-news radio stations continuously to see if there is fast-breaking information that he or his clients have to react to. In addition he reads *International Herald Tribune, Congressional Quarterly* and other informational periodicals. In essence, Garth says: There's nothing in the media that gives the pulse. *He doesn't believe there's anybody who has a message from God—no individual commentator, writer or paper.* In other words, David Garth and those like him believe in getting their opinions from other opinion makers!

So just who *are* our modern opinion makers? You'll meet them in media consultant offices, on Madison Avenue, or in Hollywood. You'll find them displaying their books in the supermarket, hosting our favorite TV talk shows, and even staffing some of the family-planning clinics! If we are not careful to filter their opinions through some vertical input from God, we will find ourselves beginning to believe, like David Garth, that there isn't "anybody who has a message from God . . . concerning the issues of today" and that perhaps, as so many people are suggesting to a conditioned public, marriage and the family are *not* such good ideas after all.

Ridicule as a Weapon

Think *how* Sanballat and his cronies attacked the builders of the walls of Jerusalem. Strangely enough, Nehemiah was not met with a barrage of rocks or stones, nor even with a vat of boiling oil, but rather with a barrage of laughs. "They mocked and ridiculed us" (Neh. 2:19). Ridicule is a powerful weapon; and Sanballat, Tobiah, and Geshem used it as soon as the children of Israel began their good work.

Nobody likes to be laughed at. People didn't like it then, and they don't like it today. For example, a teen-age boy talking with his friends might suggest that he thinks sex outside of marriage is wrong. He will in all probability be met with a fusillade of ridicule, before which it is all too easy to capitulate. Returning home, still hanging onto his principles, he may sit down to watch TV and listen to a comedian trying to make him laugh at his "old-fashioned" ideas. And then he finds that "the theme of the movie of the week is sex outside the walls—the *only* way to go!" The young man is right—God has told us that sex outside of marriage is wrong—but how can you blame him for wondering as he gets so much opposition from every direction, often in the form of ridicule.

Meanwhile his sister settles down to watch her favorite soap opera and finds herself so drawn to the likable characters who are intertwined in all sorts of adulterous relationships that she begins to accept what they do, even if they are doing what is unacceptable! She knows that God has said, "You shall not commit adultery!" and that this is one of the Ten Commandments. But Sanballat, Tobiah and Geshem have rewritten God's rules and presented them to us as the Ten Amendments, and we and our children are learning *them* assiduously!

God says lawlessness is sin, witchcraft is abomination, and sex outside of marriage is prohibited—yet three top-selling paperbacks of the 1970s were *The Godfather,* dealing with crime; *The Exorcist,* concerning demonism, and *Love Story,* which glorified fornication.

If It Feels Good . . .

Which brings us to the basis of Sanballat's philosophy. There are no absolutes, says he; right and wrong change with the times. Past is past and now is now. Maybe in days gone by it *was* right and good that Jerusalem should have its boundaries, but that was because the people who lived then didn't know any better.

We must agree with Sanballat that times *have* changed, and that we *are* now living in an experience-oriented society; but if the walls are left in a heap and we refuse to rebuild them—omitting to lay down godly principles on which *our* families will operate—then soon our rules will be mixed with the rules of the world, and our daughters and sons will not know the difference. Sanballat's line of thinking simply does away with the distinctive of Christian living. Lines are bent, good is made to look bad, and bad is made to look good whenever a "new" idea comes along. If human beings are making the rules, anyone's rule is as good as the next; but if, on the other hand, the Absolute King has drawn absolute lines and told us they are constant from the beginning of time to the "end" of eternity, then we ignore them at our peril. Especially when the same Absolute Lord tells us we will be punished if we ignore them!

Sanballat can tell us the absolutes have changed, but *saying* they have changed doesn't change them! In Romans 1 we read that people decided to change the truth of God into a lie and worship the created more than the Creator (v. 25). But *deciding* to change the truth *didn't* change it, just as deciding to believe that a gun will not kill us if we put it to our head and pull the trigger will not change the fact that it will!

Many today are telling us that if we make up our mind something is right, then it is! Or, if we *feel* it's right for us, then it must be! For this reason, some teen-agers have ended up giving in to their dates' advances and having sexual intercourse, even though they have felt terribly guilty about it. But, you see, they are experiencing guilt because they *are* guilty! God has set within each of us a conscience which tells us when we've stepped outside the walls. Remember, we are designed to be moral beings, made in the image of God, and have been lent the grand capacity to know when we have become *immoral*.

Of course Sanballat, Tobiah, and Geshem have an answer to that, too. "It's not that you've done something *wrong*," they explain to our young people; "you feel guilty because you're just not *ready* to do it yet."

Answering the query of a teen-ager who asked, "Why am I so eager to have premarital sex and yet at the same time find myself holding back?" a Planned Parenthood Association booklet gave this explanation: *"You're not ready* and it may help you to know that millions of others just about your age feel the same way! Maybe sex is not for you." In answer to another young person who asked, "How will sex affect our relationship? I mean, how would I feel about myself *afterward?* Would I feel guilty?" the booklet said:

This is pretty hard to answer in advance! But if you do have real doubts about how you'll feel towards yourself because of what you've been taught at home or at church—*MAYBE YOU'D BETTER WAIT until you can APPROACH SEX without WORRYING about feeling GUILTY.* You wouldn't want anything to spoil the wonderful experience that sex can be when it's with the right person at the right time (italics and capitals—my emphasis).

The writers of the pamphlet were not necessarily advocating marriage for the couple in question, but rather arguing that the adolescents should wait for the right time, place, and partner inside or outside the walls, and this was to be determined by their own judgment, not by God's law.

The Bible teaches us it is not a question of "Am I ready?" but "Am I right?" Further, there is not one set of absolutes for Christians and another set for non-Christians. An absolute is an absolute, and if God says sex outside the walls is wrong, then it is absolutely wrong for *everyone,* just as the rule that it's wrong to kill is a rule for everyone and not just one particular set of religious-minded people.

One day on a university campus I was approached by a young man after I had given a talk on Christian marriage. "How can you tell me sex outside the walls of marriage is wrong when it feels so good?" he inquired. He was using the argument, *If it feels good, it must be right.* I told him that human appetites will always *feel* right while we are indulging them, but the Bible tells us there are times when the right feeling can lead to the wrong actions. Chocolate chip cookies will always taste good to us, but that doesn't mean we should eat them twenty-four hours a day. There comes a definite moment when the good feeling is leading us to wrongdoing, and we have to stop.

I explained to that earnest young man that there must be controls over our appetites, sex included, and that this is logical, as we are told by the experts that one male *Homo sapiens* has the capacity to populate a small village and to "feel good" while he's doing it! So when someone says, "If it feels good, it must be right; and therefore nobody should stop me," he or she is not thinking straight. In *The Four Loves,* C. S. Lewis says that the problem is that men and women worship "love"—or, more accurately, *eros* love, the sensual "feeling too big for words." "For 'love's' sake I neglected my parents . . . cheated my partner, slept with my boyfriend," people tell us. Eros, says Lewis, extenuates, almost sanctions, *any* actions it leads to. "Love made me do it," says the woman who has stolen her neighbor's husband. There is almost a note of triumph in her voice—certainly not guilt. In Milton's words, "These reasons in love's law have passed for good."

The music that chases us in and out of our daily meanderings from supermarket to gas station and back into our kitchen, living room, and even our bedroom underlines this whole philosophy. If it feels good, it must be right; so if it feels good, *do it,* sing the songs. As our young people follow the charts, they imbibe a steady musical diet of this whole lifestyle. We need to tell them there has to be more than living by their instincts or total choas will result. Moral considerations must check and balance our desires.

Agape or Eros

Marriages fall apart because so many couples set out worshiping a "feeling too big for words" that they mistake for real love. Eros, or sexual love, needs help if it is to stay sweet; and C. S. Lewis reminds us that *agape* love needs to come to its aid. Agape love is God's sort of love and is primarily concerned with the well-being of others. It is bound to give rather than take. It promises to stay committed whether it feels good or bad. It is in effect the absolute best of love reserved by the Absolute God for those who will live within His walls and find therein space, time, safety, and fulfillment.

This is not to say eros is not of God, for God is love, and all love is of Him. But, as Lewis says, something must help mere feeling if feeling is to be fueled and develop permanency. In Lewis's day young people got married expecting "mere feeling would do for them permanently all that would be necessary"; but as the writer points out, "Eros is the most mortal of our loves and the world rings with complaints of his fickleness. In fact eros always promises what eros is not able to perform!"

Sanballat, Tobiah, and Geshem, however, continue to sell us a bill of goods, using every possible device to encourage us to worship Eros alone rather than to love, worship, and obey God.

The Enemy

Why were Nehemiah's enemies so hostile toward him? I believe they were so bitterly opposed because they were prompted by Satan himself. Make no mistake, Satan uses Sanballat—even when Sanballat himself doesn't believe in Satan's existence! Behind the furious attack on our marriages and families, we face the one who is exceedingly mad because he knows he has so little time on earth to wreak the havoc he plans (Rev. 12:12-15). We are at war with the one who laughed at the Cross (but, I would remind you, hurriedly stopped laughing at the Resurrection!). A dangerous animal mortally wounded is the most dangerous animal of all, and such is Satan, the family-hater. Nehemiah, recognizing that an unseen spiritual battle was raging around them, exhorted his fearful workers to take courage; for he assured them, "God will fight for us" (Neh. 4:20). He knew that his God was a God of battles, a God of angels, and a God of giants—a God committed to working out His purposes.

Ephesians 6 tells us we must wrestle with these unseen evil influences and do battle with the spiritual wickedness in high places (v. 12). As we do, we can remember Paul's words, "If God be for us, who can be against us?" We may even feel sorry for the enemy, for by the same token, if God be against them, who can be for them? Only the devil, and he is on the way out—defeated at the cross of Christ. God is on *our* side, and He is our Captain. He is truly the Lord God of hosts.

There was once a prophet named Elisha, who had a supernatural gift of insight. Elisha had incurred the fury of the king of Syria, who was at war with Israel, by repeatedly telling his own monarch the enemy's plans. Elisha's servant rose early one day and, going up to the top of the house, saw a great host of soldiers that had been sent to end his master's interference. "Oh, my lord, what shall we do?" the servant cried, for the soldiers were surrounding the city. He couldn't understand how Elisha could be so cool, calm, and collected about it all. Seeing the young man's distress, the prophet asked the Captain of the hosts of heaven to open the frightened man's spiritual eyes so he could see what he himself had been able to see all the time. God answered that prayer, and the astonished servant saw the armies of heaven and their fiery chariots all around them. "Don't be afraid," said Elisha. "Those who are with us are more than those who are with them."

The battle for the boundaries *is* raging, but the battle is the Lord's, and those who are with us are more than those who are with them. So take courage. We *are* on the winning side!

Worksheet

A. *The Battle*
  1. Who are our enemies? Review Ephesians 6:11-12.
  2. Where do our modern Sanballats, Tobiahs, and Geshems get their opinions from?
  3. Discuss the following:
     a. The methods they use to spread their ideas.
     b. The way ridicule is used by the media to attack Christian values.
     c. What is humanism?
     d. What are absolutes? Do you agree that modern society asks us to live by the Ten Amendments rather than the Ten Commandments?
     e. What would you say to a young person who says, "If it feels good, it must be right"?

B. *The Boundaries*
  We need to know the biblical limits of our sexual relationships.
  1. *Sex inside the walls*
     a. Write out Hebrews 13:4 in your own words.
       Note: This does not mean that "anything goes" in the bedroom once we are married. Sex without love is lust. Sex governed by love results in blessing and joy. Christian marriage must not be based on sex but on a commitment to a covenant of which sex is only a part. Sex should not be used as a weapon but rather as a sweet expression of our love for each other and our oneness in Him.
     b. Read aloud Ecclesiastes 4:8-12. List the things this passage can teach us about marriage.
  2. *Sex outside the walls*
     a. Sex outside the walls often leads to a disintegration of the relationship we are trying to keep intact. In *Letters to Karen,* Karen, writing to Walter Trobisch about giving in to her boyfriend's sexual demands, grieves about the termination of their relationship: "I can't understand it. I didn't want it but he did. When I gave in, he lost interest. For him, it was the end—for me it was the beginning."
       (1) Write a one-page letter to Karen from a biblical perspective, explaining why premarital sex caused the end of her love affair.

        (2) Discuss within your group the advice you have given to her.

  b. Fornication is sex outside the walls.

        (1) *Pornos* is the root word from which "fornication" comes. What does this word remind you of?

        (2) The word *fornication* is used in the Bible to describe both premarital sex and extramarital sex, i.e., adultery. Write down what these verses teach us: Ephesians 5:3; Matthew 15:19; 1 Thessalonians 4:3.

  c. Adultery is sex outside the walls.

    Adultery violates the law of love, for if we love our neighbor as ourself, how can we then covet another's wife or husband? Write out Exodus 20:14.

  d. Homosexuality is sex outside the walls.

        (1) The Book of Romans describes unrepentant homosexuals as people God has given up to uncleanness (1:24, 27-32).

        (2) Read Leviticus 18:22; 20:13 and 1 Corinthians 6:9-10, then answer the following questions:

            (a) What does God call homosexuality?

            (b) How do we know what He feels about it?

3. *God's view of sex*

  a. Read 1 Corinthians 6:9-20. and write down what you learn from these verses about: God, Christ, the Holy Spirit, your body, the act of sex, fornication, and God's forgiveness.

  b. Remember that God forgives the sinner who repents of all sins, whether sexual or otherwise.

C. *The Blessing*

This week read the Song of Solomon devotionally and pray about the battle for the boundaries.

THE BUILDERS

3

The Watchers: Prayer

When our enemies heard that we were aware of their plot and that God had frustrated it, we all returned to the wall, each to his own work. From that day on, half of my men did the work, while the other half were equipped with spears, shields, bows and armor. The officers posted themselves behind all the people of Judah who were building the wall. Those who carried materials did their work with one hand and held a weapon in the other, and each of the builders wore his sword at his side as he worked (Neh. 4:15-18).

To do your work with one hand while holding a weapon with the other is not the easiest way to build a wall! However, being the man of prayer that he was, Nehemiah prayed as he worked and watched for the enemy. Throughout the book we read his troubled prayers (1:4), his telegram prayers (2:4), his terrible prayers (4:4-5), and his true prayers (1:5-11). He believed that builders were pray-ers. When his brother told him about the great trouble and disgrace of God's children, Nehemiah turned to prayer—not as a last resort, as we so often do, but as a seemingly practiced and natural reflex.

What do *you* do with bad news? How do *you* react when your brother brings you some distressing information about the people you love? Do the shock waves drive you to say stupid things or force you to pick up the phone and spill out the story to someone else, hoping that in some mysterious way passing on the information will somehow offset the hurt you are experiencing? Maybe you are too stunned to react in any way, and morning finds you moving mechanically about the duties of the day. Perhaps your defense is a flurry of activity or, if you are of English heritage, the soul-saving ritual of brewing a cup of tea!

Preparation for Prayer

Nehemiah's response bears examination. The Bible tells us that it was some time before Nehemiah eventually got around to true intercession, some *days,* in fact, before he could even formulate a "proper" prayer. I take great comfort from this information. It helps me to know that it took Nehemiah time "to do it right," especially when you consider the fact that he was supposed to be an "expert." (If we had to taste the king's brew every day to see if it was poisoned, we would be expert pray-ers too!) You see, before this beautiful, articulate, organized, and effective request popped out of his mouth, Nehemiah had to calm down. *Praying about what to pray about* is an extremely necessary part of the preparation for prayer, for God must deal with our emotional reactions before He can trust us to ask Him for the right things.

As we look more closely at Nehemiah's preparation for prayer, we can learn many things from him, one of them being that it's all right to cry! Yes, even if you are a believer! "When [Nehemiah] heard these things, [he] sat down and *wept"* (1:4). I know some people who think they have failed as followers of Jesus if they ever shed a tear. "Christians don't cry," a lady with a tight smile informed a friend of mine at a funeral. "Then how come Jesus wept?" my friend muttered into her handkerchief! "Tears talk; God hears. The Bible tells me so!"

In Psalm 56:8 we read: "Put thou my tears into thy bottle: are

they not in thy book?" (KJV). When I think of tears, I think of
God's bottle and His book, then I weep "happily" in the knowledge that it's all right to cry!

In the psalmist's day, a family mourning their dead would weep
over a wineskin, "putting their tears in a bottle"! Then they
would carefully carry their "grief" and place it at the tomb of the
loved one. I thought about those tears—

Tears talking,
    pattering petition on the door of heaven—
        Let me in.
Wet misery,
    fountains of fury,
        rivers or recriminations—
tears tearing down the riverbed of doubt—
        stopping at the throne.
Bottled bereavement,
    arranged by angels,
        given to the King!
God tilts the bottle carefully over His book
    of remembrance,
        letting the drops fall onto a clean page.
Transported in a teardrop,
    translated into eloquence,
my washing woe writes its words of wounded
    worry down.
Splashing sadness signs its name;
    then dry depression comes to stay,
        for all the tears have gone.
The Father reads my tears,
    passes the book to the Son,
        who shares it with the Spirit.
The angels gather round.
    Some small celestial cherubs
        are lifted to the Father's knees:
           The story is told.

They listen.
They all listen.
I am heard!
"I have heard her prayers; I have seen her tears,"
says the Father.
"I am touched with the feelings of her infirmities,"
says the Son.
"I will pray for her with groanings which cannot be uttered,"
says the Spirit.
"And God shall wipe all tears from her eyes,"
sing the angels.
"And there shall be no more death
Neither sorrow nor crying,
Neither shall there be any more pain,
For the former things shall pass away!"

Yes, it's all right to cry; for when we are emotionally upset, our prayers may spring from panic or desperate selfishness, and in that hurting moment we may find ourselves demanding a particular response from God that we would certainly be sorry to receive. We should thank God that He doesn't always answer our angry demands. Sometimes, in the face of such need, we should simply sit down, mourn, weep, and "be" a prayer. Notice, I said, "be" one—not "say" one.

Have you ever awakened in the middle of the night weighted with worry, dead with dread, yet utterly unable to bundle up all that heaviness into a relaxing and releasing petition? Next time dawn finds you so hopelessly inarticulate, don't even try to talk. Lie still and let your very body language say to God, "Lord, I *am* a prayer. Read me!" Then as morning comes and you go about the jobs that must be done, try silently lifting your spirit to Him, saying in effect, "Lord, I *am* a walking prayer. See me. Help me!" He can hear the language of our worry just as clearly as He hears the wailing of our words. And He has promised that He will give us a garment of praise for the spirit of heaviness (Isa. 61:3 KJV).

I remember receiving the bad news that our daughter had had an accident. I was far away from home at the time, and my immediate response was to press the panic button, demanding some dramatic action from God. "Lord, get me out of here and take me to my little girl," I prayed. "She needs me, *so You have to do this!"* Running to the camp office to make travel arrangements, I discovered there was no way I could leave that place for at least two whole days. Back to God I marched to implore Him to "Send a whale, Lord—a couple of ravens—a fiery chariot—anything, so long as it moves. You can do it. I know You can! *Please!"*

Then the tears came. At first it helped, but when the tears were done, a heavy despondency dressed my spirit. There were no more words—I *was* a prayer. After fasting all day, I was finally able to pray rightly; I requested that Judy would learn to lean on her heavenly Father, since she couldn't lean on her earthly parents. As she was enrolled "in the school of hard knocks," I asked that she would only be knocked down, not out, and that one day she would even be glad we hadn't been able to be there! God answered those prayers, although it took many years to do so. But then, who said anything about *my* "now" being *His* "now"? He has His own "proper" time to hear and answer our petitions.

In God's proper time a way was provided for Stuart and myself to travel home to our injured child—but not before His purposes had been accomplished and she had graduated from the "school" of hard learning with a high grade in faith. (Perhaps we need to spend some time thinking back over the years, thanking God for all the prayers He *hasn't* answered!)

Pattern for Prayer

After we have taken time out to pray about what to pray about—*we have to start to pray about it!* We could call the first part of prayer "the waiting part" and the second part "the working part," for—make no mistake about it—prayer *is* work. Effective prayer takes effort, time, and discipline. This is the side of intercession that often has a discernible "pattern" to it. In the first chapter of the Book of Nehemiah we see a grand example of this.

O Lord God

Nehemiah reminded himself of Jehovah's character by beginning his communication with the Almighty with the words, *O Lord God. . . ."* We cannot get down to the business of petitioning God without an adequate vision of Him. And the more knowledge we have concerning the nature of the Father, the more confidence we will experience as we approach His throne. What we know of His character determines what we expect of Him and, on the other hand, what we *don't* expect of Him!

It was the voice of the Lord God (Jehovah Elohim)—the Eternal Seeking One—that called out to lost humanity in Eden, "Adam, where are you?" Understanding the constancy of the redemptive nature of God, Nehemiah felt free to ask Him to come calling all over again, this time saying in effect, "Israel, where are you?" Now Nehemiah had only his knowledge of the Father to give him encouragement, whereas you and I have had added revelation concerning the Son and the Spirit to strengthen *our* hearts. When God came to earth in Christ to reconcile the world to Himself (2 Cor. 5:18-19), He reaffirmed His redemptive character through the life and work of Jesus of Nazareth.

Do you remember how Jesus, finding one more sinner hidden up yet one more tree, invited Zacchaeus to come down and face Him? "Zacchaeus," He said, "come down immediately. I must stay at your house today" (Luke 19:5). *But what has all this to do with my family and my prayer life?* you may ask.

Perhaps you have a husband who is just like Zacchaeus—a businessman whose line of work or position in his company means he is not particularly popular with the employees. Maybe he has even made some of his money by sailing pretty close to the wind, but when challenged, replies, "When you're dealing with the Romans, you have to do as the Romans do!" Perhaps like Zacchaeus your husband has even sought to "see" Jesus. He has been to church with you and seems open to understanding what commitment to the Lord is all about. If I had a husband like that and was praying for him to meet the Christ I had met, I would start my prayers with the words, "O LORD God," reminding myself of Jehovah and how He came in Christ "to seek and to save what was lost," namely all the Zacchaeus's down the ages. I would gain great confidence and boldness as I remembered Jesus stopping under Zacchaeus's tree, knowing He could do it again. Then I would certainly encourage my heart with Christ's marvelous words, "I must stay at your house today." You see, it's what we know about God's "constant" character that keeps us praying and believing He will act on our behalf!

Or perhaps you have a child who has rejected God. You can be assured of the Father's will in this matter because He has already revealed it to us. Christ told us, "Your Father in heaven is not willing that any of these little ones should be lost" (Matt. 18:14). He also promised us that the Father would hear and answer any prayer that was in accordance with His will. He told us that the Good Shepherd *goes after* that which is lost. What a comfort to know that as far as your child is concerned, when you cannot "go after" him any more, the Good Shepherd is busy doing just that. You can know this because He has told us, "Jesus Christ is the same yesterday and today and forever" (Heb. 13:8).

And the Christian can be assured that the Holy Spirit is also at work. This seeking Spirit knows no boundaries or barriers. Some of my favorite words were penned by the psalmist in Psalm 139 concerning the Spirit of God: "Whither shall I go from thy spirit? or whither shall I flee from thy presence? If I ascend up into heaven, thou art there: if I make my bed in hell, behold, thou art there. If I take the wings of the morning, and dwell in the uttermost parts of the sea; Even there shall thy hand lead me, and thy right hand shall hold me" (Ps. 139:7-10 KJV).

Years ago, while working among young people from the back streets of Liverpool, I was able to start a Bible class for them. They were hardly conversant with the Scriptures yet were thoroughly conversant with the Lord. Some of them could not even read. One day as I was reading these verses from Psalm 139 to them, I asked if anyone could put them into his or her own words. After a long pause, one of the boys looked up and said, "I guess it means God's got longer legs than I have!" I guess it does, doesn't it?

There is no place we can run to that is outside the permeating influence of the seeking, striving Spirit of God.

Can you begin to see that what we know of the character of the Lord from the Word of God assures us that we have come to the right *place* and to the right *Person* with our prayers?

Great and Awesome

The next element of Nehemiah's prayer had to do with the Eternal's ability. "O LORD, God of heaven, *the great and awesome God,*" he prayed. In the midst of some pretty awe-inspiring circumstances it helped to talk with a God to match! Nehemiah thought about the power of the Lord to move the minds of the kings of the earth, to manipulate politics, and even to move a whole population where He would!

> Remember the instruction you gave your servant Moses, saying, "If you are unfaithful, I will scatter you among the nations, but if you return to me and obey my commands, then even if your exiled people are at the farthest horizon, I will gather them from there and bring them to the place I have chosen as a dwelling for my Name" (Neh. 1:8-9).

Whenever our families are in trouble and we need to kneel and pray, we must believe the God we speak with has the *power* to move mountains, men, monarchs, and even mothers-in-law if need be! Just to rest in a God who can motivate the unmotivated and move the immovable will prove to be a heart-releasing experience. We need to practice a continual trust in this "awe-ful" God, especially when we've been waiting for something to give in a certain situation. Perhaps we've even been patient for many years and feel we have grown old with hoping. We must come to understand that delay may be telling us that God is not necessarily saying "not ever," but simply "not now."

Think of the man who patiently waited beside the pool of Bethesda (John 5). He had been lying there for thirty-eight years, watching for an angel to appear, ruffle the waters, and attend to his needs. During his lonely vigil there had been some heavenly manifestations in that place, but no one had helped him down into that healing pool. He had watched God answer other people's prayers, but never his own. But God *had* heard his prayers, and He *did* move in that man's life—in His own time.

> When Jesus saw him lie, and knew that he had been now a long time in that case, he saith unto him, Wilt thou be made whole? The impotent man answered him, Sir, I have no man, when the water is troubled, to put me into the pool: but while I am coming, another steppeth down before me. Jesus saith unto him, Rise, take up thy bed, and walk. And immediately the man was made whole, and took up his bed, and walked (John 5:6-9 KJV).

Just think what that man would have missed if God had merely sent an angel instead of coming Himself in the person of Christ to heal him. Oh, how we long to see a moving of the waters and our loved ones made whole; but we have to realize it is all a matter of the timing of God and *not* a question of whether He hears and answers prayer. I am not saying that God will always heal "when" we ask Him to or "the way" we ask Him to, but I do believe that prayer for healing *always* gets answered eventually, even if we have to wait until He takes us to heaven to enjoy it!

It is not a matter of *can* God, but *will* God, and if He *will*, "when" He wills is His business and not ours. In other words, don't lose faith in the ability of your awe-inspiring God just because the waters don't move the moment you tell Him to move them!

Who Keeps His Covenant

The third thing Nehemiah thought about as he prayed was the fact that the Lord he loved was a covenant-keeping God: "O LORD, God of heaven, the great and awesome God, *who keeps his covenant* of love with those who love him and obey his commands," he prayed (Neh. 1:5). God was committed to keeping His promises, and Nehemiah clung to that and the fact that some of Jehovah's servants were fulfilling the conditions for the blessings he sought. He knew he could claim God's promises if at least a few of His servants were being obedient, so he prayed boldly, "O Lord, let your ear be attentive to the prayer of this your servant and to the prayer of your servants who delight in revering your name" (1:11).

We may as well save our breath if we are busy praying for things God has never promised us. But He has said, "If you remain in me and my words remain in you, ask whatever you wish, and it will be given you" (John 15:7). This is His covenant with us. God has obligated Himself in grace to accomplish certain announced purposes; and if we will but cooperate with Him, we will find out that He is as good and as great as His Word.

While my children were living through their turbulent teenage years, I avidly studied the book of the prophet Isaiah. I marked the places in my Bible where God promised blessings to His people and *to their children* if they would only follow Him. I noted other promises of God as well, and since I was struggling at the time with the whole dating issue, one verse in particular arrested my attention. It had to do with the city of Jerusalem: "Like birds hovering overhead, the LORD Almighty will shield Jerusalem: he will shield it and deliver it, he will 'pass over' it and will rescue it" (Isa. 31:5). The time had come when I could no longer "hover" to defend, protect, and preserve my children. I had to let them go out on their dates all alone! Reading this Scripture and applying it to my anxious heart, I said to myself, "If the Lord God will do this for His *city,* how much more for His *child!*" The next time the "dates" dated, I sang this little refrain over and over again: "As birds hovering, passing over, I will preserve, and defending I will deliver." I was not claiming a promise He had not made or was unable to keep, but rather a promise He had stood behind in the past and was well able to perform in the present.

I Confess

Having been prompted by his vision of God, Nehemiah was able to take a true look at himself and his family. Then, as praise leads naturally to penitence, he was quick to confess his shortcomings, saying, *"I confess* the sins we Israelites, including myself and my father's house, have committed against you" (1:6b). This was the sorrow of a godly man! "Godly sorrow brings repentance" (2 Cor. 7:10), and Nehemiah demonstrated true repentance, the essence of which is not sorrow that we have been caught, but true sorrow for our sin.

People who are truly sorry for their sins will want to do something about it! They will seek a way to make some sort of restitution—at any cost! Taking his very life in his hands, Nehemiah asked the Lord to "give [him] success . . . by granting him favor in the presence of [the king]" (Neh. 1:11b). True repentance always leads to action, and here we can see the pattern: prayer—penitence—petition, and what a bold petition at that. How could hope be born in one so hopeless and seemingly helpless to help? Well, prayer changes things, people, circumstances, and even attitudes. It makes possible the impossible. Without prayer Nehemiah would have been tempted to conclude that since he was a slave, that was that; but after time with God in preparation and then in intercession, he had come to believe that He who was Creator, Jehovah, Elohim, the Great and Awesome One, was well able to hear the petitions of the penitent. Placing his reliance in the Lord God whose ear he believed was attentive to his requests, Nehemiah opened his mouth and asked for the moon—receiving it in his lap!

So we have seen Nehemiah *praying about what to pray about,* and we have seen him *praying about it.* Finally, we shall observe him *praying about what he has prayed about!*

Persistence in Prayer

After Nehemiah had arrived in Jerusalem and had gathered the leadership together, you will remember that Sanballat, Tobiah, and Geshem, the officials of the place, appeared on the scene. They continually gave crafty council to Nehemiah's other enemies and sought by all means at all times and in all ways to hinder progress. Despite their efforts, the remnant who "had a mind to work" (KJV) began to see the completion of the walls. Now all that remained to be done was the setting up of the doors in the gates.

> When word came to Sanballat, Tobiah, Geshem the Arab and the rest of our enemies that I had rebuilt the wall and not a gap was left in it—though up to that time I had not set the doors in the gates—Sanballat and Geshem sent me this message: "Come, let us meet together in one of the villages on the plain of Ono." But they were scheming to harm me; so I sent messengers to them with this reply: "I am carrying on a great project and cannot go down. Why should the work stop while I leave it and go to you?" Four times they sent me the same message, and each time I gave them the same answer (6:1-4).

In verse 9 we find Nehemiah praying about all this intrigue: "They were all trying to frighten us, thinking, 'Their hands will get too weak for the work, and it will not be completed.' But I prayed, 'Now strengthen my hands.'" After any victory we will need to keep in close touch with God. Nehemiah prayed, "Now, Lord, strengthen my hands"—strengthen them to follow through, to finish what has been begun, to hold the ground that has been gained. All that takes tenacity we are going to have to pray about!

If you think it is hard to pray in crisis, I want you to know it is harder still to keep praying when the crisis is through! To pray when everything is going wrong can be a sort of forced necessity, but to pray consistently when everything is going all right is another thing altogether! The problem is that we can be lulled into self-complacency concerning the attitude of the enemy. We can come to believe there is a deescalation of his activity and fall into a false sense of security. "Come, let us meet together . . . come, let us confer together," suggested Nehemiah's opponents (6:2, 7).

The adversary of our souls and of our families will never be laid off. He will never "go soft" on us. "They were scheming to harm me," says Nehemiah, wisely discerning his enemies' intent (6:2). Knowing his foes so thoroughly, this man of God realized the opposition would never change their goals, just their strategy. So it is with us today. We can know that Satan, who is behind every destructive attack on the family structure, will never change his goals; but he will certainly change his strategy. Watch, therefore! I believe if we do not know how to "pray on" after the family trouble is over, we will simply lurch from crisis to crisis.

Not long ago I counseled with a teen-ager. She was greatly disturbed and confused because her parents were talking about getting a divorce. I promised I would pray about the situation and told her to keep in touch. A few weeks after our conversation, when the immediate problem had been resolved, she pressed the following piece into my hand:

> I saw my family
> Falling apart.
> I didn't want it to!
> So I sought help and advice
> From a friend.
> It was given to me:
> I must fight for my family
> Like never before
> Until they're solid on their feet.
> That meant giving sacrificially at times, at others,
> Taking a stand on my convictions.
> Now the crisis seems to be over,
> But I'm finding that
> It's necessary to continue fighting
> If another crisis has any chance
>   of being avoided.
> That's gonna take a lot of doing!

She was only a young teen-ager, but she was an "old" disciple, don't you think?

It is necessary indeed to continue praying if another crisis is to be avoided! There is only one word that describes this sort of praying—persistence! This is praying when we don't *feel* like it—it's keeping on keeping on when we're tired out with the huge emotional strain of our recent confrontation.

So often we do not finish what we start. And if we are undisciplined in other areas of our lives, we will, in all probability, be undisciplined in our prayer life too. Let me give you a practical hint: this week try to finish something you have left unfinished. Work on some sewing or painting, complete a letter, or paint the fourth wall of that room! Take up jogging once again, or finish reading that novel. Start to "follow through" on these lesser things, and then you'll be ready to work on your prayer life. Don't try to do it yourself, though—make sure you pray about it all! If you don't know how, I'm sure Nehemiah wouldn't mind if you borrowed his words: "Lord, now strengthen my hands."

The best illustration of this can be found in a story in Exodus 17:8-15. Amalek had been Israel's avowed enemy for years. Joshua was busy fighting him in the valley, while Moses stood on a hill overlooking the battle. Moses held the rod of God, representing God's authority, in his hand, and while he held the rod high, Israel prevailed. But when his arms grew tired and he let them fall, then Amalek gained ground! Hur and Aaron, who were standing beside God's great prophet, took a big stone and asked Moses to sit on it. Then they positioned themselves on either side of him, supporting or "strengthening" his hands with theirs. Then, the Bible tells us, Israel won the day!

God has many ways of strengthening our hands in prayer. Sometimes He gives us His own unseen support, prompting us to keep on praying that the enemy may be held at bay. At other times He lends us the hands of brothers and sisters in the body of Christ, His church, and we are blessed with a corporate support system. How ever He does it, our persistent prayer will always be answered, for Jesus Himself told us we "should always pray *and not give up.*" (Luke 18:1).

Worksheet

A. *Preparation: Praying about what to pray about*
Reread Nehemiah 1:1-11.
"When I heard these things, I sat down and wept. For some days I mourned and fasted and prayed before the God of heaven" (1:4).
1. *Tensions:* reactions and responses to crisis
   a. Imagine yourself in a tension-filled Super Bowl. Your team is losing—badly! There is very little time to save the situation. Knowing yourself as you do, answer these questions:
      (1) Who do you see yourself as (E.g., coach, fan, quarterback, treasurer of the club, weeping owner)?
      (2) How would you *like* to see yourself react in this situation (E.g., as a cheerleader)? Share your honest answers with the group.
   b. Think of some family crisis and try to remember your reactions. (E.g.: When a crisis happens in my family, I immediately become a spectator. I seem incapable of refereeing or any useful action.)
2. *Time:* waiting on God
   Why do we need to take time to pray about what to pray about?
   a. Each person take one of the following verses and put it in his or her own words: Psalm 27:14; 37:7; 40:1-3; 130:5-6; Isaiah 40:31; 64:4; Lamentations 3:25-26.
   b. Discuss the *reasons* for waiting and the *promises* to those who do, as found in each particular Scripture verse.
3. *Tears:* "It's all right to cry."
   a. After looking up these references, discuss questions:
      (1) Ecclesiastes 3:4: What place do tears have?
      (2) Genesis 23:2; 27:38; 43:30; 2 Samuel 19:1; Ezra 3:12; Nehemiah 1:4; Psalm 69:10; Luke 19:41; 22:62; 2 Corinthians 2:4: Are tears for women only?
   b. Write out in your own words: Psalm 30:5; 116:8.
B. *Pattern: Praying about it*
   1. Review Nehemiah 1:5-11. What pattern did Nehemiah use as he prayed?
   2. Read Isaiah 6:1-8 and make an outline of the pattern of Isaiah's prayer.
C. *Persistence: Praying about what you've prayed about*
"Now, [Lord,] strengthen my hands" (Neh. 6:9).

1. Concerning follow-through, discuss:
   a. The deceiver's devices.
   b. The disciples' disciplines.
   c. Which area of prayer (A, B, or C above) do you find most difficult and why?
D. *Prayer Time*
   1. Share one family prayer need with your partner.
   2. Pray for each other.

4

The Man With the Trumpet: The Holy Spirit

Then the Jews who lived near them came and told us ten times over, "Wherever you turn, they will attack us." Therefore I stationed some of the people behind the lowest points of the wall at the exposed places, posting them by families, with their swords, spears and bows. After I looked things over, I stood up and said to the nobles, the officials, and the rest of the people, "Don't be afraid of them. Remember the Lord, who is great and awesome, and fight for your brothers, your sons and your daughters, your wives and your homes." When our enemies heard that we were aware of their plot and that God had frustrated it, we all returned to the wall, each to his own work. From that day on, half of my men did the work, while the other half were equipped with spears, shields, bows and armor. The officers posted themselves behind all the people of Judah who were building the wall. Those who carried materials did their work with one hand and held a weapon in the other, and each of the builders wore his sword at his side as he worked. *But the man who sounded the trumpet stayed with me.* Then I said to the nobles, the officials and the rest of the people, "The work is extensive and spread out, and we are widely separated from each other along the wall. Wherever you hear the sound of the trumpet, join us there. Our God will fight for us!" So we continued the work with half the men holding spears, from the first light of dawn till the stars came out (Neh. 4:12-21).

Having lent himself to the purposes of God, Nehemiah requested divine help in carrying out those purposes. He tells us in a metaphor that "the gracious hand of my God was upon me" (2:8), meaning that he accomplished the work "by the agency of the Lord."

In the Book of Acts we read about the "hand of the Lord" getting "a grip" on people's lives, and this happens in various ways. I could tell you the day and the hour the Lord got a grip on my life, and you could tell me a totally different story of how He laid His hand on you; but essentially we would be saying the same thing. We would be testifying to the fact that there came a moment when *the man who sounded the trumpet—the Holy Spirit—came to us!*

The Man With the Trumpet Comes to Us

In the Old Testament, the Holy Spirit came upon whom He would and departed at will. When Jesus lived on earth, however, He told His disciples that at Pentecost the Spirit would come to impart to many what previously had been the privilege of the few. So it came to be, and the Spirit ceased to be an occasional supplier of God's power and help for certain individuals in specific situations; He became instead an uninterrupted sustainer of the supply of God's energy and power in the church universal.

Has the man with the trumpet come to you? Perhaps you were raised in a churched family, brought up in a Christian tradition, and it seems as if you have always known the Lord. Maybe you cannot remember the exact day, hour, or year that He laid hold of you. The important thing is not that you remember the exact time, but that there was such a moment when this occurred. Is He with you now? Is there evidence of His presence in your life? You can not mistake the indwelling presence of the Holy Spirit any more than you can mistake the sound of the trumpet! There are unmistakable evidences of His occupancy that prove He has indeed come into your heart to stay.

The Man With the Trumpet Calms Us

Nehemiah, experiencing a sense of isolation as he walked around those walls all by himself, could surely have testified to the differences as the solid, stable shape of the man with the trumpet came into view. He could have explained it somewhat poetically in this fashion:

> *I heard the grand vocabulary of His steps*
> *along the wall,*
> *echoing in my ear,*
> *mellowing the fear,*
> *saying it all—*
> *"I'M COMING!"*
> *The melody of His approaching*
> *embroidered His arrival with*
> *stitched sounds,*
> *colored strands of comfort,*
> *Sewing serenity across my apprehensions,*
> *saying it all—*
> *"I'VE COME!"*

Those of us living in this day and age can look back to Calvary, the Resurrection, and the Day of Pentecost and know that when we received the Holy Spirit, He came into our hearts *to stay.* Nehemiah could only know the temporary certainty of the Spirit for his specific task. Even King David found it necessary to pray, "Take not thy Holy Spirit from me" (Ps. 51:11 KJV). For you and me, however, it is gloriously different, for Jesus promised us that "when" the Comforter would come, *He would abide with us forever.* Listen to Jesus telling His disciples about the One who would be coming when He would be going: "And I will ask the Father, and He will give you another Counselor to be with you forever" (John 14:16).

The Man With the Trumpet Comforts Us

Nehemiah undoubtedly rejoiced in the companionship of the man with the trumpet. How glad he must have been for the man's presence during those dark and dangerous days as they kept watch over God's family together. I am sure the man with the trumpet brought Nehemiah great consolation. This type of heavenly companionship is one of the evidences of the Spirit's indwelling—an inner assurance, deeper than emotion, that convinces us we are never alone—even when humanly speaking we are!

Furthermore, when the man with the trumpet comes to us, we find that He is not only company, but *good* company! He brings with Him a sense of stability as He inhabits our souls, and we find we are "content with what [we] have, because God has said, 'Never will I leave you; never will I forsake you'" (Heb. 13:5). So the person who wonders if he or she has ever received the Holy Spirit in the first place has to ask this question: "What do I know of this constant Helper who has the ability to touch the raw edges of my inner hurts and whisper that healing is on the way? Do I really know what it is to be content with what I have or what I have not because I have Him?"

Jesus put it another way, saying that when the Holy Spirit comes to stay, people feel like orphans who have been adopted! "I will not leave you as orphans; I will come to you," He promised (John 14:18). Do you feel like an orphan? As if you don't "belong" to anyone even if you have ties by name to a particular family? Then maybe that's because the man with the trumpet has never come into your heart!

One of the things I noticed as soon as I accepted Christ by His Spirit was a strange, "belonging" sensation somewhere deep down inside my personality that told me God was settling in forever! What a Guest! And what a rest as well. As I discovered freedom from constantly seeking human relationships that would deal with that awful orphan feeling, I was able to stop shouting silently to no one in particular, "Hey, who's listening? I need to matter to someone who matters to me!" When the man with the trumpet comes to stay in us and comfort us, then the foundling is found and it's all right from then on, wherever we go or whatever occurs.

We don't really know if any other Jewish brothers had been taken captive with Nehemiah, or if he had any fellowship or support in the king's palace, but the evidence seems to point to the fact that he was a practiced "loner." A loner—and yet never alone! If we had been able to watch him going about the duties of the day around the palace, we would probably have noticed that there wa͜ something different about him, something we couldn't quite put our finger on. You see, when people are indwelt by God, they give the distinct impression that they are always deep in conversation with an unseen friend.

I remember lying in hospital, having a conversation with the girl in the bed next to me. I had the wierdest sensation that while I was talking to her, *she* was talking to someone else, even though there was not another person in sight! (After I had invited the same sweet Companion who lit up that young woman's life to light up *my* life, I understood about the quick, "wordless" conversations one can have about other human beings, even while you are talking to them!) As we conversed together in that hospital ward, I knew with some uncanny sense that I was being discussed with "Someone Else." It was infuriating! Afterward I learned that what was actually happening was that the Holy Spirit was teaching her to pray for me.

> In the same way, the Spirit helps us in our weakness. We do not know what we ought to pray, but the Spirit himself intercedes for us with groans that words cannot express. And he who searches our hearts knows the mind of the Spirit, because the Spirit intercedes for the saints in accordance with God's will (Rom. 8:26-27).

If we are in a state of shock after we have received some traumatic family news—or if we are busy mourning, weeping, and praying about what to pray about—it certainly doesn't mean there is nothing going on! The Holy Spirit is busy going on! He has never been, nor ever will be, shocked or surprised. Furthermore, He does *not* need to pray about what to pray about. He *knows* exactly what needs saying, and He's already hard at work saying it. What a comfort to know that the people in need will not be deprived of blessing until we get around to praying. The Holy Spirit "helps" our weakness while at the same time presenting the Father with a true and right request from His loving heart.

The Man With the Trumpet Copes for Us

Another thing the man with the trumpet does is to help us cope. Not just to survive, but to cope—with hope! When Nehemiah asked the man with the trumpet to stay with him, the situation they faced was extremely dangerous. In fact 4:21 tells us that the people continued the work . . . from the first light of the dawn till the stars came out. Neither Nehemiah's servants, nor the men of his guard, nor he himself put off their clothes except to wash (4:23). This was probably the most difficult, exhausting and frightening time of all, for no one was sure just where the enemy would strike.

Listen to Nehemiah exclaiming somewhat desperately, "The work is extensive and spread out, and we are widely separated from each other along the wall" (4:19). The only comfort Nehemiah had at this point was the presence of the man with the trumpet. But it was not just his companionship that helped, for the man with the trumpet was specially equipped with abilities to see in that sinister darkness and was therefore able to impart a sense of simple confidence as he encouraged everyone to believe he could alert them to "cope" with an attack by the enemy. In similar manner, the Holy Spirit helps us to "cope with hope," in the New Testament sense of the word hope—overwhelming confidence.

Having called the man with the trumpet to his side, Nehemiah began to give instructions to the people. "Wherever you hear the sound of the trumpet, join us there," he told them (4:20). He knew that they could be summoned by the man with the trumpet whenever necessary! Notice I said whenever necessary. The Holy Spirit does not summon reinforcements without reason! He draws divine attention to our plight only when He sees that we need it. Then He acts, blowing an instant heavenly alert, and we find ourselves mysteriously and strangely helped!

I think of Corrie ten Boom, who was used to help so many Jewish people hide from the Nazis during the days of the Holocaust in The Netherlands. In her book, *The Hiding Place* she tells how, caught by the Germans, she found herself on board a train traveling toward a concentration camp. Frightened, yet courageous, she thought of her father and a conversation they had had when she was just a little girl. At that time she had expressed the fear that she would never have the courage to be tortured for her faith. In reply, her father had asked her a question: When was it that he gave her a dime for a bus ride? "Just before I get on the bus," she had answered. "So it will be with God," her father had explained.

It is the man with the trumpet who will provide the currency, but only when it's time for the money to be spent!

I wonder what it was like to be one of Nehemiah's busy builders during those days of harassment. They must have cultivated a consistent attitude of awareness. As they held a sword with one hand and worked with the other, both ears must have been cocked in the direction of the man with the trumpet. What tense expectation, what willingness to listen, and what sweet readiness to be the first to return to Nehemiah's side.

The Man With the Trumpet Cares for Us

I like to think about our brothers and sisters in Christ who have labored along the wall and been attentive to the Spirit's call, some of them separated from us by very great distances. One particular incident stands out in my mind. It was the year our daughter Judy graduated from high school. Our graduation gift to her was a trip around the world with her father as he visited many mission fields and ministered to the missionaries. Off she went in high spirits, though a little apprehensive about their first two weeks that were to be spent in Bangladesh and India. And I got down to pray every night, trusting the Lord for all the things you can imagine a mother would need to trust Him for in such a situation!

Unbeknown to me, Judy contracted a strange virus and became extremely ill. Way out in a remote part of Bangladesh she began to run an extremely high temperature that could not be treated because of the absence of drugs. While my daughter was so sick in that isolated place, I was in Milwaukee sleeping like a baby! Far away "along the wall," however, on the continent of Africa, there labored another mother. She was a missionary's wife whom I had met when she was home on furlough and whom I had been able to encourage. Seeking to encourage me in return, she had promised to pray for our children. The same night I was fast asleep unaware of my daughter's plight, all those hundreds of miles away "the man with the trumpet" came to my friend's side and blew an insistent note right in her ear! Alerted, she began to pray for Judy!

For a few days following this experience, a heavy necessity hung about her, driving her to intercede even though she had no idea what was wrong. Then the burden lifted! She became absolutely convinced that all was now well and that a beautiful relationship was developing between Judy and her father! She hadn't been in touch with me for quite a while *and had no idea Judy and Stuart were even on a trip together!* But the man with the trumpet made sure He summoned her just when Judy needed help. She sent me a letter telling me about her experience, but neither of us knew till the travelers returned just what it had all been about!

Never underestimate what the Holy Spirit is doing for your family through the ministry of prayer while you lie fast asleep. On the other hand, we all need to learn a lesson from the builders and begin to listen for the sound of the trumpet with a new urgency so that we may go to the aid of some brother or sister who desperately needs our support!

The Man With the Trumpet Convicts Us

Now the man with the trumpet doesn't just alert us to other believers and their prayer needs; He alerts us to the movements of the enemy as well. One of the things I noticed as soon as I came to know Christ was the strange inner alarm system that had apparently been mysteriously and secretly installed. Thinking about it now, it sounded suspiciously like the sound of a trumpet! It was certainly a note one could *not* ignore. For example, a few days after my conversion, I was talking to some of my friends. I had not had an excessively dirty mouth, but then I had not been famous for having a clean one either. As the conversation flowed along some irrelevant course or other, I suddenly became aware of the rather shady language that was flowing quite naturally out of the aperture under my nose. And I was listening to it because I had been alerted somehow, somewhere, by that heavenly Trumpeter, who had blown a blast of caution right into my mind! As the days progressed, I continued to experience an increasing awareness of the enemy's presence and received a direct challenge from within whenever I allowed him inside the walls!

When young Christians ask me, "How will I know if I am doing something wrong?" I usually tell them, "You'll know. There's something unmistakable and unforgetable about the sound of the trumpet."

As we fight for our families, we need to understand the ongoing ministry of the man with the trumpet. We dare not ignore His warnings. We must not treat Him with benign neglect. He is sent to us by our gracious Father as a "Helper," One whose work it is to strengthen and encourage us.

Has the man with the trumpet come to you? Does He indwell you, comfort you, alert you to danger, and constantly warn you of your sin? If all this makes no sense to you, it may just be that He has never come to you in the first place. Maybe this is because you simply do not know "how" to call Him to your side. You want Him, and you know you need Him, but you wonder just how you two can get together. Is that the problem? Then let me help you.

The Man With the Trumpet Converts Us

When I lay in hospital listening to Janet, the girl in the next bed, telling me about her man with the trumpet, I remember experiencing an immense and overwhelming longing. If only I could know Him, too, I thought. But I didn't know how to "connect," and I didn't like to ask my new friend to help me in case she thought me stupid for not knowing how myself!

I thank God from the bottom of my heart that Janet saw my predicament and said to me, "Jill, what's the matter? Don't you know how to ask Him in?"

"No, I don't know," I mumbled sheepishly.

"That's okay. I didn't know how either until someone told me," she replied cheerfully. "Let me help you," she continued. "I'll say a prayer inviting Him to come into my life, and you can 'borrow' the words and make the prayer your own." And so she did. And so I did—and He came as Jesus promised that He would, to abide with me forever!

If you like, I'll do the same for *you* right now, and you can borrow *my* words even as I borrowed Janet's. Quiet your soul, climb into a still point wherever you happen to be at this very moment, and say:

> Lord Jesus, I hear Your Word teaches that if anyone does not have the Spirit of Christ, he or she is no Christian. Quite honestly, I do not know for certain if You have ever come to abide in my heart. I am mixed-up and confused about the whole issue. So because I'm not sure if You live within me, I would like to make sure—right now! Please, Lord, by Your Spirit come to me, enter me, comfort me, and witness to *my* spirit that You've moved in to stay. Forgive my sin, alert me to the enemy, and from this day forth teach me how to pray. Amen.

Now, if you have borrowed these words and truly meant them, He *is* indeed *your* very own Companion and Helper. You can begin to rely on Him to supply you with all the strength that you will need as you fight for your family. The Holy Spirit will continue to blow His blasts at your sin down through the years; He will draw your attention to an arrogant attitude, a selfish tantrum that you may dress up self-righteously, or anything that grieves His holy heart. He will alert you to sins of commission as well as to sins of omission. He will take away many a hungry ache for human companionship, provide you with an insatiable zest for life, for service, for witnessing, and for building the walls! You will grow to love Him and praise Him for sending you "the man with the trumpet," and not until you get to heaven will you ever know the extent of your debt of gratitude for His gracious work on your behalf.

Worksheet

A. *Review*
  1. Review Nehemiah 4:12-21.
  2. Who can the "man with the trumpet" represent?
  3. Explain the term "the hand of the Lord" (Neh. 1:10; 2:8b; Acts 11:19-21).
  4. Share some evidence of the Holy Spirit's occupancy in your life.

B. *Study*
  Work through the following study in a group. Each person may complete a section, then share his or her findings. (The following study is taken from *Discovering God* by D. Stuart Briscoe, excerpted from *Getting Into God* [Grand Rapids: The Zondervan Corporation, 1975], pp. 37-41. Used by permission.)

  1. *The Holy Spirit is a Person.*
     (1) *Which personal acts does He perform?*
A. John 14:17	D. Acts 13:4
B. John 16:13	E. Romans 8:26
C. Acts 13:2	
     (2) *Which personal attributes does He display?*
A. 1 Corinthians 12:11	C. 1 Corinthians 2:13
B. Romans 8:27	D. Romans 15:13
     (3) *How did Christ speak of Him as a Person?*
A. John 14:16	B. John 14:17
     (4) *How is it possible to treat Him as a Person?*
A. Acts 5:3	D. Ephesians 4:30
B. Acts 5:9	E. Hebrews 10:29
C. Acts 7:51	

  2. *The Holy Spirit is God.*
     (1) *By which divine titles is He called?*
A. Genesis 6:3	E. Matthew 10:20
B. 2 Chronicles 15:1	F. Romans 8:9
C. Isaiah 11:2	G. Galatians 4:6
D. Isaiah 61:1	
     (2) *Which divine attributes does He display?*
A. Hebrews 9:14	D. Psalm 139:7-10
B. 1 John 5:6	E. 1 Corinthians 2:10
C. 1 Thessalonians 4:8	
     (3) *Which divine tasks does He perform?*
A. Job 26:13	C. John 3:5
B. Matthew 12:28	

(4) *In which great events did He participate?*
    A. Genesis 1:2   D. Hebrews 9:14
    B. Matthew 1:18-20   E. Romans 8:11
    C. Luke 4:1   F. 2 Peter 1:21

3. *What are the Holy Spirit's qualities?*
    A. Romans 1:4   G. 2 Corinthians 4:13
    B. Isaiah 11:2   H. 2 Timothy 1:7
    C. Zechariah 12:10   I. Hebrews 10:29
    D. John 14:17   J. 1 Peter 4:14
    E. Romans 8:2   K. Isaiah 4:4
    F. Romans 8:15

4. *What are the symbols of the Holy Spirit?*
Look up the following verses and note the symbols. Why do you think that particular symbol was used? (E.g., in John 3:34 and Heb. 1:9 the symbol is oil. In Scripture, oil symbolizes the anointing of royalty; joy.)
    A. John 7:38-39   D. Matthew 3:16
    B. John 3:8; Acts 2:2 E. Ephesians 1:13; 4:30
    C. Acts 2:3   F. Ephesians 1:14

C. *Personalize*
Look up the following verses and choose one of the aspects of the Spirit's work that you need to appropriate in your immediate family situation.
1. His convicting work (John 16:7-8)
2. His converting work (John 3)
3. His convincing work (Rom. 8:16)
4. His consoling work (Rom. 8:15)
5. His constraining work (2 Cor. 5)

D. *Prayer time*
1. What is *one* thing you have learned from this study that you can put into practice this week?
2. Use this period for some silent prayer and some corporate prayer.

5

The Priests and Levites: The Word and Worship

Eliashib the high priest and his fellow priests went to work and rebuilt the Sheep Gate. They dedicated it and set its doors in place, building as far as the Tower of the Hundred, which they dedicated, and as far as the Tower of Hananel. . . .
> Next to him, the repairs were made by the Levites under Rehum son of Bani. . . .
> The repairs next to him were made by the priests from the surrounding region. . . .
> Above the Horse Gate, the priests made repairs, each in front of his own house (Neh. 3:1, 17a, 22, 28).

Nehemiah, nobles, nobodies, and even the priests and Levites —everyone went to work rebuilding the walls. When that project was finished, it was time to construct something even more significant than the protective boundary that had been designed to shield the family from the enemy without. The cement of regular worship and the Word of God was needed to protect them from the enemy "within." The priests and Levites can represent to us these two vital, protective elements of the Christian life—the Word and worship.

We read in Nehemiah 7:73 that the "priests, the Levites, the gatekeepers, the singers, and the temple servants, along with certain of the people and the rest of the Israelites, settled in their own towns." At this point no one would have blamed the children of Israel for enjoying a bit of well-earned R and R, but their leaders were cognizant of the fact that until some spiritual issues had been settled in their hearts, the people would never be able to truly settle down in their homes. And thus it was. "When the seventh month came . . . all the people assembled as one man in the square before the Water Gate. They told Ezra the scribe to bring out the Book of the Law of Moses, which the LORD had commanded for Israel" (7:73b-8:1).

The Liberating Law

In Ezra 7:8-9, the book immediately preceding the one that we are studying, we read about "Ezra the scribe." He had arrived in Jerusalem because "the good hand of his God was upon him." Well-versed in the law of Moses, he served the heathen King Artaxerxes, who acknowledged him to be a "teacher of the Law of the God of heaven" (7:21). This same monarch gave Ezra power to appoint magistrates and judges to administer justice to all the people of the Trans-Euphrates and to teach them God's laws. If any appeared reluctant to learn their lessons, Artaxerxes, in typical Persian fashion, ordered their "death, banishment, confiscation of property, or imprisonment" (7:26). It is no wonder that with such a powerful opportunity Ezra had taken courage, gathered leading men of Israel to go with him, and had arrived in the Holy City praising God, who had "put it into the king's heart to bring honor to the house of the LORD in Jerusalem in this way" (7:27).

It appears that first and foremost Ezra was a man of the Book—or rather the scroll! War, killings, and slavery had not interrupted his glad, intense desire to study God's Word and flesh it out through his godly character so that those around him in like captivity might experience a freedom of the heart. Whenever I think of this godly man, I am forcibly reminded of the words of the psalmist: "I will walk about in freedom, for I have sought out your precepts" (Ps. 119:45).

The existence of law (in this case, God's law) leads to a profession whose business it is to study and grasp its meaning. In Ezra's day it was the job of the priests to so examine and interpret the Holy Writings; but as time went on, a class of scholars developed who were not priests themselves, but who devoted themselves to be guardians of the sacred Scriptures, professional students of the Law. These men were called *scribes.* Ezra, acknowledged as priest *and* scholar, was such a man. He was "learned in matters concerning the commands and decrees of the Lord for Israel" (Ezra 7:11).

I cannot help wondering just when the Law of the Lord had leaped to life for Ezra. Yet one thing *is* certain: by the time we meet this scholarly scribe in the Scriptures, he had already become a hunter of heavenly gold, the discovery of which had invested him with celestial wealth, encouraging him to rejoice that he was indeed a child of the King! I have a vision of this man amid the brassy business of forced labor, yielding meek obedience to harsh orders issued by larger and yet lesser men, stubbornly rehearsing David's words:

> Your statutes are wonderful; therefore I obey them. The entrance of your words gives light; it gives understanding to the simple. I open my mouth and pant, longing for your commands. Turn to me and have mercy on me, as you always do to those who love your name. Direct my footsteps according to your word; let no sin rule over me. Redeem me from the oppression of men, that I may obey your precepts. Make your face shine upon your servant and teach me your decrees. Streams of tears flow from my eyes, for your law is not obeyed (Ps. 119:129-136).

What joy Ezra must have felt—to be given leave to return to Jerusalem with authority and power to teach his greatly loved precepts to chastened Israel and, to have a part in rebuilding the temple and reestablishing national worship.

Let me pause here and ask: Do you regard the law of the Lord as sweet as honey or as sour as soap? Have you, like Ezra, dis-

covered this heavenly treasure chest or are you perhaps uncon-
vinced regarding this precious paradox—the wonderful freedom
that we experience as we allow ourselves to be bound tightly with
the cards of inquiry to God's liberating law? Maybe you are
asking yourself, "How can law be liberating?" In my younger
years that was my own quandary as I reasoned that true freedom
must mean every person "doing that which was right in his own
eyes." And yet, I had no answer for the fact that in the exercise
of this so-called liberty, regardless of accountability to God,
man, or beast, I sensed a tightening bondage of spirit squeezing
the very liveliness out of me. This liveliness I regarded as my
rightful heritage, a sort of inalienable right to be happy however I
chose to live! It was only as I subjected myself to the liberating
obedience of the law of the Lord that I found myself singing
aloud, "Your statutes are my heritage forever; they are the joy of
my heart" (Ps. 119:111).

As I walked out of the dusky darkness of disobedience, I found
that His Word became "a lamp to my feet and a light for my
path" (119:105) and that indeed "the entrance of [His] words
gives light" (v. 130). I also discovered that He illuminated my
stupidity with sound knowledge as He gave "understanding to
the simple" (me!) and His statutes became my counselors. Even
when I was "laid low in the dust," He renewed my life according
to His Word (v. 25). And when my soul was weary with sorrow,
He strengthened me (v. 28)!

It was tough to admit that I had swallowed the devil's suggestion that God's laws were bad because they were restrictive; but
once I had confessed that fact, I found myself in wholehearted
appreciation of a conclusion Ezra would heartily have concurred
with: His laws are *good,* and He has laid down precepts that are
to be *fully* obeyed. I discovered that if we are seeking a full life of
blessing, there is no easy way to find it. We must fully obey if we
are to be fully blessed! And that is never easy! I meet many
Christians who are upset with God because they are not satisfied
with their lives. When I inquire how fully they are obeying Him,
they look at me in amazement. They say, in effect, "Let Him first

fully bless me; *then* I may get around to some obedience." But that is not how it works. We cannot barter with God. We must not issue any demands at all, for we are but diminutive dust parlaying with omnipotent Deity. We should want to obey because we have intellectually come to the conclusion that His law is *good* and *right*.

Living God's Word

With the burning conviction—that the family in Jerusalem needed to be instructed anew concerning God's law—Ezra sought to reintroduce worship into the nation's life, apparently encountering no resistance from the people. In fact, they very quickly rallied around him. Perhaps it was simply that they did what he said because he said what he did!

What an example Ezra gives us! How can we expect our children to read their Bibles if we never blow the dust off ours? How can we reasonably require church or Sunday school attendance from our little ones if their father "worships God" on the golf course? If God is no more important than a golf ball, who can blame a child from dropping the whole Christian curriculum? It is high time for the fathers of our families to return to Jerusalem and rebuild the temple.

I believe that a true discovery of the Word of God leads to a devoted dedication in the study of it. This in turn will lead to a determined effort to demonstrate it in one's life, which hopefully will have the end result of a balanced transmission of it to one's family. As parents, we have the great responsibility of dispensing that marvelous spiritual fare that has become our own most necessary meat and drink. But if we are not living it out, our children will most probably reject it outright, and we can hardly blame them for that. Once I overheard a woman asking a friend whose preaching had brought about her conversion. "No one's preaching," she replied. "It was Aunt Mary's practicing!" Just so. To discover the Word of life is one thing; but if we do not demonstrate the truth of it in our behavior, then it doesn't 'live' at all.

Paul, writing to the Corinthians, says proudly of these new Christians, "You show that you are a letter from Christ, the result of our ministry, written not with ink but with the Spirit of the living God, not on tablets of stone but on tablets of human hearts" (2 Cor. 3:3). Can this be said of us? Are we living epistles that anyone can open and read? Or would we have to admit we would prefer to keep our letters in their envelopes?

Preaching and Teaching

Having greeted Nehemiah and the next contingent of returning exiles with great joy, Ezra must have delighted in throwing his considerable spiritual weight behind the building project; and I am quite certain that some years later he would not drag his feet when summoned to read his beloved law of the Lord to the people at the Water Gate.

Now to be devoted to the Word is one thing, but to be able to deliver it effectively and publicly to others is another thing altogether. Every Christian is a witness, but not every believer is a preacher or a teacher. God has gifted some of the body of Christ for such a ministry, and it behooves those who have been so gifted to think about Ezra carefully and glean some relevant lessons from his experience. First of all, look at the mechanics of his preaching.

> So on the first day of the seventh month Ezra the priest brought the Law before the assembly, which was made up of men and women and all who were able to understand. He read it aloud from daybreak till noon as he faced the square before the Water Gate in the presence of the men, women and others who could understand. And all the people listened attentively to the Book of the Law. Ezra the scribe stood on a high wooden platform built for the occasion. . . . All the people could see him because he was standing about them (Neh. 8:2-4a, 5b).

First, then, we learn that Ezra was visible and vocal. I remember being told that the three rules of public speaking were—stand up to be seen, speak up to be heard, and shut up to be appreciated! Mechanics *are* important, though obviously not all-important. How thankful I have been over the years to the people who have constructively criticized my manner and method of teaching. I remember many occasions during my training in the secular field that I was required to instruct my class in front of an advisor from my college who sat at the back of the room and took copious critical notes. Why not expect a similar evaluation from the church? One of our problems is that most of us have a weakness in our own characters that stubbornly resents being criticized. We should abhor such selfish response, for surely we desire to be our very best for the Master. I believe the church should have courses for teachers, not only in what to teach, but in how to teach it.

Having invited a gifted teacher of the Book to take the pulpit, the people settled down to listen. Notice who was there that day: "the men, the women and others who could understand." In other words, the children were there as well. The whole family was worshiping together.

We have lost the concept of family worship in much of the Christian education of today. We insist on separating the different age groups until we never set eyes on another member of our own family circle from the moment we put our feet inside the door on Sunday morning to the moment we leave.

"But the adult service is boring for our children," some object. "And it's too long for the very little ones," argue others. Church certainly took a long time the day Ezra read the Book of the Law at the Water Gate, for we read: "He read it aloud from daybreak till noon"; and yet we notice that "all the people listened attentively to the Book of the Law." It does no harm to require attention on occasion from our children—at least those who are old enough to understand. You may rest assured that no one has ever died of boredom!

The secret is in the phrase "on occasion," for you can see from the text that on the second day only the adults gathered for Bible study. "On the second day of the month, the heads of all the families, along with the priests and the Levites, gathered around Ezra the scribe to give attention to the words of the Law" (8:13).

Following this adult learning period, the whole family celebrated the Feast of Tabernacles, and *that* was *fun*.

> So the people went out and brought back branches and built themselves booths on their own roofs, in their courtyards, in the courts of the house of God and in the square by the Water Gate and the one by the Gate of Ephraim. The whole company that had returned from exile built booths and lived in them. From the days of Joshua son of Nun until that day, the Israelites had not celebrated it like this. And their joy was very great. Day after day, from the first day to the last, Ezra read from the Book of the Law of God. They celebrated the feast for seven days, and on the eighth day, in accordance with the regulation, there was an assembly (8:16-18).

What child would not enjoy listening to Bible stories while camping out in rooftop tree houses! So I am not saying, "Make sure your kids are dragged to church and bored out of their minds every week." But I am suggesting that it does no harm to require family participation "on occasion." All normal children will probably go through an I-don't-want-to-go-to-church phase. It can happen at any age and in any family, and our own experience has been that it happens most regularly at the junior-high stage. With the rush toward independence comes a push away from church.

I well remember meeting our youngest head-on on one such occasion. An hour before worship began, he announced with grand finality, "I'm not going!"

We had a visiting preacher staying with us at the time, and he happened to be sharing the program with my husband. Overhearing this remark, he said, "Come on, Pete. I'm going to have a bit of fun with your dad tonight. I'm going to be giving him his introduction!"

Without pausing, Pete replied, "My dad doesn't need an introduction—he needs a conclusion!"

His underlying message was—"It's too long; it's too boring; and I know it all." Furthermore, he had realized he was taller than his mother, and she couldn't *make* him go!

Somehow I won the battle of wills and got him to church, but on the way I was conscious that Pete wasn't the only one with a problem! I had to admit I was more concerned about what people at church would say if our son didn't turn up than I was about my child's struggle. What would the flock think of their "model" Christian mother and her little wayward lamb? That day on the way to Sunday worship, God dealt with my heart; He gave me a proper concern for our son and a willingness to share the problem with a trusted friend so that she could pray.

Stuart talked openly with Pete and took the pressure off by telling him that while he was a member of our family and living in our house, he would be required to be in the Lord's house on the Lord's Day—and also in Sunday school, but on "occasion" he could have an evening off! This did the trick and focused Pete's attention on the concession rather than on the expectation.

Next I investigated the program being offered by our fellowship and found it necessary to drop some of my other activities to help with creating a more meaningful opportunity for Pete's difficult but delightful junior-high age group. We called them the "God Squad" and put the emphasis on teen involvement and participation rather than on expecting them to listen to yet another Bible story that by now they could probably tell as well as the teachers! Having found the church program invigorating and cheerful, we had no further problem requiring our son's attendance; and by allowing him concessions here and there, the heat was taken out of the situation.

We found that involvement, responsibility, and a challenge to leadership are the keys to relieving boredom every time. When that same child struggled with Sunday school in upper high-school years, we put him to work in a Christian athletes study as a junior leader. Similarly, our daughter (growing out of Sunday school) found a place teaching in the kindergarten department. It was a great encouragement for me to read Nehemiah 8 and find out the family in Jerusalem followed a similar pattern: requiring attendance, giving leeway at certain times, and in general making learning a fun, family experience.

Add to this the goal of having the right man in the pulpit with the right gift, doing it the right way, and you have a winning combination! Ezra was vocal, visible, and viable, and the results were dramatic. The people of the family of God returned to the Lord in repentance and faith, showing the reality of their renewal in acts of contrition and obedience.

The mechanics and the method of disseminating truth are indeed intriguing to study. Ezra and the Levites "instructed the people in the Law while the people were standing in front of them. They read from the Book of the Law of God, making it clear and giving the meaning so that the people could understand what was being read" (8:7-8). Nehemiah also took part in this instruction (v. 9).

After the reading, the crowd was either divided up into manageable "classes" or the teachers took turns applying the Word of God to the people's lives (the meaning of the text is unclear). Whatever method was used, the ministry was shared by a band of men whose hearts the Lord had touched. Ezra was obviously not threatened by other spiritually gifted men, but seemingly enjoyed the team spirit. No attitude of competition spoiled their fellowship as each took turns ministering to the people. The teachers' goal was obvious: "that the people could understand"!

Communication, it has been said, is only communication when the hearer as well as the speaker has grasped the full meaning of the truth taught. To have such receptivity, there must be not only gifted teachers teaching, but a preparation of the people's hearts before the Word can be fully assimilated. That preparation is worship.

Familiar Yet Fresh

Ezra opened the book. All the people could see him because he was standing above them; and as he opened it, the people all stood up. Ezra praised the LORD, the great God; and all the people lifted their hands and responded, "Amen! Amen!" Then they bowed down and worshiped the LORD with their faces to the ground (8:5-6).

I know churches where people come only to "hear the Word." They arrive late, saying by their tardiness that they disdain "all that waste of time before the real stuff begins"! I am sure that this is abhorrent to the Lord. We must have a prepared spirit if we are to receive His directives. Worship prepares us to hear the hard things God intends us to hear. Worship is His by right; it is something we can do for Him before He does something for us, and to deny Him our praise is little short of an insult! Worship really means "worthship" and is our personal acknowledgment that He is indeed "worth something" to us. Surely we must come to meet with the Lord in a spirit of humility and gratitude.

Having all things in order, Ezra opened the Word of the Lord in such a way that a fresh touch of the Spirit of God motivated the people of God to active obedience. The message was familiar, yet somehow fresh. It was Samuel Johnson who said, "Men need rather to be reminded than instructed." In other words, it is often the things that we already know that we need to pay attention to rather than some truth we have never heard before. As the leader of Israel searched the familiar Scriptures,

> They found written in the Law, which the LORD had commanded through Moses, that [they] were to live in booths during the feast of the seventh month and that they should proclaim this word and spread it through their towns and in Jerusalem: "Go out into the hill country and bring back branches from olive and wild olive trees, and from myrtles, palms and shade trees, to make booths"—as it is written (8:14-15).

Now everyone already knew about this feast; but suddenly they decided it was time not only to be reminded of it, but to observe it. "Doing" the truth makes the difference. We can sit under the preaching of the Word of God, saying to ourselves, "I know all this," and miss the whole glorious point because we never mix it with faith and make it ours. Next time you listen to a sermon, ask yourself, "Am I *doing* this?" Obedience will fan the familiar into a flame of freshness.

I remember one Sunday when I was sitting in church feeling miserable because I was on a motherhood guilt trip. Our eldest child had just gone to college, and I was wandering down the lonely labyrinth of self-analysis that invades a mother's heart at such a time. I was busy mourning all the stories I hadn't read to him, all the games we hadn't played together, all my lack of interest in his homework, the favorite foods I had seldom taken the time and trouble to cook for him—you know, all those "mother sins" that refuse to be laid low by reason.

That day I was not a little irritated to hear Stuart begin his sermon on the grace of God. I had heard him preach that message many times before. In fact, it was so familiar that I probably could have preached it myself. "Why couldn't he choose something that would help me with my problem?" I asked the Lord petulantly.

"Why don't you try listening instead of griping?" He answered.

"But I don't need to listen," I argued. "I *know* this. I understand about the grace of God covering all my sin! I have thanked You many times for cleansing me from all my iniquity. You found and forgave me—I know that!"

"And what about all your sins since you became a Christian?" the Lord inquired. "There is grace to cover *all* your 'mother sins'!"

Swell! Shattered into silence, I sat quite still, suddenly and completely overwhelmed by the all-prevailing grace of God to me. Yes, it was indeed a familiar truth, but, touched by the Spirit, a fresh flame of warmth brought comfort to my mind and the joy of the Lord flooded in. That fresh touch upon the familiar is the Spirit's business. This is that mighty meddling with our souls in which the living Lord delights, working in us a resultant holy hilarity. Listen to Nehemiah and Ezra telling the people:

"This day is sacred to the LORD your God. Do not mourn or weep." For all the people had been weeping as they listened to the words of the Law. Nehemiah said, "Go and enjoy choice food and sweet drinks, and send some to those who have nothing prepared. This day is sacred to our Lord. Do not grieve, for the joy of the LORD is your strength." The Levites calmed all the people, saying, "Be still, for this is a sacred day. Do not grieve." Then all the people went away to eat and drink, to send portions of food and to celebrate with great joy, because they now understood the words that had been made known to them (8:9b-12).

An applied understanding of God's Word involves a weeping over the familiar and a joy in the fresh—a celebration of the lifting liberation of God's power in response to our repentance and faith.

In Matthew 13:52 Jesus explained to His disciples that "every teacher of the law who has been instructed about the kingdom of heaven is like the owner of a house who brings out of his storeroom new treasures as well as old." Another translation of "new treasures as well as old" gives us "the familiar and the fresh"! There it is! We who are New Testament "scribes" need to practice bringing the familiar and the fresh out of the precious inexhaustible storehouse of the Word of God! This thought has had a marvelously freeing impact in my life and ministry. As I stand in front of the same class every week I have been delivered from feeling I have to produce something brand-new every time I teach. I seek instead to impart a fresh application of the familiar.

I love the way this passage ends in joy. The Feast of Tabernacles was instituted so the Israelites might remember that they had been "brought out to be brought in." The Feast of Tabernacles was to remind the people that God had brought them out of Egypt into Canaan. The idea of living on the top of their houses in booths made of tree branches was intended to bring to mind their pilgrim heritage and God's great faithfulness during those wilderness wanderings. For seven days the families were to live on top of their houses enjoying a grand time of reminiscing and rejoicing.

The priests and Levites of Nehemiah's day were not one bit afraid to take the Word of God literally and apply it practically to their family living. The end result was celebration—and so it will be for all of us who dare to do the same. There is a strength in spiritual joy. It is a power that the world cannot reproduce synthetically, an irritating puzzle to the nonbeliever, and a vibrant witness to a jaded and lost humanity. Finally, the joy of the

Lord is the strength we need to function in our families according to His Word, and that joy cannot become ours apart from an obedient, submissive spirit. When we are inwardly submissive to the Lord who is all joy, we will be outwardly and gladly obedient.

Worksheet

A. *Review*
1. Read Nehemiah 8-9:3.
2. Who was Ezra (Ezra 7:8)?
3. What had he done in Jerusalem before Nehemiah arrived?
4. What was his testimony in captivity (Ezra 7:6, 25-26)?
5. What was his mandate from the heathen king?
6. Ezra *discovered* the Scriptures, was *devoted* to them, *demonstrated* them, and *dispensed* them. Which of these words describes you at the present time and why? Discuss.
7. Discuss this statement of Scripture: "His laws are good and He has laid down precepts that are to be fully obeyed."
   a. Do you agree that we must fully obey if we are to be fully blessed?
   b. Look up the following examples: Numbers 14:24; 1 Kings 11:1-11.
8. Talk about the *mechanics* and the *method* Ezra used as a teacher (Neh. 8:2-3, 5-7).
9. His message was familiar yet fresh. What was the result (8:9-12)?
10. Read each of the following texts. Pray about each and ask God to give you a fresh thought—a new application from a familiar text. Share it!

Luke 1:45	James 4:17
Luke 4:39	Psalm 104:32
Romans 1:14-15	Psalm 23:1
2 Corinthians 5:10	John 3:16
2 Thessalonians 3:13	

11. Discuss:
    a. the reasons why children don't want to go to church
    b. the ways parents make them go
    c. the parents' responsibility in this matter
    Share helpful ideas about ways to achieve the desired result.

B. *Remind*
Work through the following study. (This study is taken from *Discovering God* by D. Stuart Briscoe, excerpted from *Getting Into God* [Grand Rapids: The Zondervan Corporation, 1975], pp. 9-11. Used by permission.)

1. How does the Bible describe itself?
   a. Luke 8:11
   b. Psalm 119:105
   c. Jeremiah 23:29
   d. Ephesians 6:17
   e. Psalm 19:9-10
   f. 1 Peter 2:2

2. From your answers above, what do you think the Bible should do in your life?

3. With what subjects does the Bible deal?
   a. Philippians 2:16
   b. Ephesians 1:13
   c. Acts 13:26
   d. 2 Corinthians 5:19
   e. Hebrews 5:13

4. What did Jesus say about the Word of God?
   a. Matthew 4:4
   b. Matthew 22:29

5. What ought I to do with the Word of God?
   a. Isaiah 34:16
   b. 2 Timothy 2:15
   c. Psalm 1:2
   d. Acts 17:11
   e. Psalm 119:140
   f. Luke 24:45
   g. Psalm 119:9
   h. Psalm 119:11
   i. Acts 11:16
   j. Hebrews 4:2
   k. James 1:22
   l. John 8:31

6. In what way is the Bible of value to me?
   a. 2 Timothy 3:15
   b. John 20:31
   c. 2 Timothy 3:16
   d. Psalm 119:9
   e. Psalm 119:11
   f. Psalm 119:130
   g. Romans 15:4
   h. 1 John 5:13
   i. 1 Peter 2:2

7. How is it possible to abuse the Word of God?
   a. Mark 7:13
   b. 2 Corinthians 2:17
   c. 2 Corinthians 4:2
   d. Titus 2:5
   e. 1 Peter 2:8
   f. Revelation 22:18-19

8. Learn the following verses and references by heart.
   James 1:22
   John 20:31
   Psalm 119:105

C. *Reflect*
   1. What was the source of the people's joy in Ezra 8:9-12?
   2. What is the source of your joy?

THE BARRIERS

6

The Horse Gate: When Conflicts Arise

After the wall had been rebuilt and I had set the doors in place, *the gatekeepers . . . were appointed* (Neh. 7:1).

The wall of Jerusalem may have been rebuilt, the people regrouped, the leadership of the family reestablished, but there were still sources of weakness to be found. The gates provided the enemy with a constant opportunity for infiltration, and knowing this, Nehemiah paid particular attention to the making of the doors and the bars. After these were set in place and dedicated, the gatekeepers were appointed.

I believe that the Christian has been appointed to be God's gatekeeper—called to stand guard at the weak spots, ready to defend the family at any cost. Six of the Jerusalem gates provide us with graphic illustrations of potential gateways of grief.

When the army left the city of Jerusalem to do battle with the foe, they passed through the Horse Gate. Therefore, I would like to use this gate to picture the place of conflict in the family.

If disputes are not dealt with promptly and properly, wounds may result that can never be healed. Because many people simply

91

do not know what to do or say when family conflicts arise, Satan uses this opportunity to exploit the situation, causing irreparable harm. Yet think of Joseph's last recorded words in Genesis 50:19, when he told his brothers, "You intended to harm me, but God intended it for good to accomplish what is now being done, the saving of many lives."

Conflicts Over Favoritism

The family-hater, Satan, lurks behind the arguments that all of us experience in measure, seeking to manipulate situations to accomplish his own evil ends. In Joseph's case, he had been shown rank favoritism by his father and from that small beginning the enemy of relationships found ready cooperation among Joseph's brothers to engineer Joseph's slavery, incarceration, and—but for the grace of God—his death! *But God intended it for good!* He always desires to use potential family conflicts for the saving rather than the destruction of lives. Instead of listening to the one who wishes us evil, we should learn, like Joseph, to respond to Him who seeks only our good.

Let's turn now to Nehemiah 5:1-6:

> Now the men and their wives raised a great outcry against their Jewish brothers. Some were saying, "We and our sons and daughters are numerous; in order for us to eat and stay alive, we must get grain."
>
> Others were saying, "We are mortgaging our fields, our vineyards and our homes to get grain during the famine."
>
> Still others were saying, "We have had to borrow money to pay the king's tax on our fields and vineyards. Although we are of the same flesh and blood as our countrymen and though our sons are as good as theirs, yet we have to subject our sons and daughters to slavery. Some of our daughters have already been enslaved, but we are powerless, because our fields and our vineyards belong to others."
>
> When I heard their outcry and these charges, I was very angry.

In other words, there was a good old family row! We hear about a fight within—not outside—the city walls, a conflict of personalities, a clash of wills, a mounting hostility between brethren. Some of the children of Israel were being shown favors, and the parents of the children who were not began to get upset about it. They became extremely angry about such partiality, for as they put it, "Our sons are as good as theirs!" How we need to guard against favoritism in the family. In Romans 2:11 we have a model of the perfect Father, who shows no favoritism; yet many of us would have to confess distinct and abject failure at this very point.

Have you ever noticed how children possess a great sense of what is "just"? "It isn't fair!" comes the plaintive cry as they clamor for our attention to the matter. My husband used to say that it wasn't really their sense of fair play that stimulated such vehement protests; what they were *really* saying was, "Hey, I lost the advantage!" This may well be so, but it is still a fact that children readily discern favors shown to siblings.

Those of us with college-age children are well-versed in the objections voiced over privileges extended to the youngest still left at home—privileges they were never permitted to enjoy. Often this sort of "favoritism" is simply the result of lessons learned by the parents on the first or second child, some wiser hindsight, or maybe just a matter of a liberalizing of our attitudes. Rank favoritism, a deliberate damaging partiality, is another thing altogether!

What parent has not experienced a clash of personalities with one or another of his or her children before the child-rearing process was through? These problems usually occur with the child who is most like oneself, the simple reason being that we see our own shortcomings in that child at some specific point of his or her development. This has nothing to do with ceasing to love them, but is a matter of disliking them for a season, which will pass as surely as the cycle of nature. While the season is with us, however, it can easily result in the parent's showing continual and irritating favors to the offending child's brothers or sisters. Such favoritism that *does not* soon pass away can result in serious rifts of relationship, not only between parent and child but also between child and child. "You love Bob more than you love me," cries a little one in preschool distress; while an older child may retire into hostile silence, seeking to "punish" his adult tormentors into noticing how much it all hurts. Even when the parent tries desperately hard to be impartial, problems can still occur; so how much more damage is done when a parent makes no real effort at all to act in a fair and reasonable way?

Can you imagine such things going on "within the walls" of God's family? Maybe you can imagine it all too well because you, too, have been caught in cruel conditions that have exposed you to rank favoritism or money-grabbing relatives. Perhaps you have had to bitterly battle your way through an ugly court case as your spouse has taken you for everything he or she can get, leaving you incapable of caring properly for yourself or your children. Sadly, such things have been known to happen.

If we guard the gateways of favoritism and moneylending, the two main causes of grievances among the folk in Jerusalem, we will then find we will have gone a long way in preventing some of the wars "within the walls" that Satan means for evil. This is not to say we should not help our own or that these are the only causes of conflict among relatives. There must surely be as many potential trouble spots as there are families themselves; but if we can start to identify sources of weakness and at the outset of hostilities ask the Father for a turning of the particular situation to good, we may well see the plans of the devil thwarted and be halfway to winning the war God's way.

Family Conflict Is Normal

Let's think about the Christian's role in the place of family conflict, using Nehemiah as our example. Half the problem when war is declared and the battle commences—whether it be an argument in the bedroom, living room, or even over the use of the bathroom—is that Christians are only human! We have feelings like everyone else, and most of us find it harder to be Christians at home than anywhere else on earth. Therefore, we need to work hard on our reactions as soon as the great outcry begins (as it usually does to a greater or lesser degree in *all* normal families).

Yes, first we must realize that conflict *is* normal. I remember the time Stuart and I were invited to write a book about teen-agers.

"We can't do it of course," I said emphatically.

"Why not?" my husband inquired.

"Well," I hesitated, "shouldn't we wait till the kids are pretty well perfect before we offer advice to the rest of the world?"

"You mean bide our time until they are all spiritual giants?" my husband asked.

"Well, yes!" I replied.

"Giants are freaks," he commented, "and I for one don't want freaky children. I just want normal ones!"

That was a most helpful statement for me. Sometimes in our great desire to see our children develop spiritually, we get very solemn and intense, demanding abnormal behavior from our youngsters, often forcing them into pretending to believe what *we* want them to believe, or behaving as we want them to be-have, just to please us. We need to relax a little and stop at-tributing spiritual problems to a child who is merely exhibiting the normal wear and tear of the natural growth process.

When to Intervene

Well, then, you may ask, if a certain amount of family conflict is normal, just when *do* we intervene? I notice with interest that Nehemiah waited until there was a "great outcry" before he stepped in to mediate the mess. I am sure he was not altogether unaware of the events leading up to the eruption, but I think he had been giving the combatants time to resolve their own dis-putes. We can try to do the same with much of the rough and tumble of childhood fun, frolic, and fighting that we witness— that is, I may add, as long as none of the parties is in any real physical danger. But there does come a point where such natural "rough and roll" becomes a bigger thing than a passing pout, hurt ego, or temper tantrum. Then, like Nehemiah, it will be our privilege and opportunity to step in and play advocate. I believe Christians are called to follow in their Savior's steps when possible, and that means being peacemakers. Jesus was called the Prince of Peace, and we who belong to Him should bear the family likeness. Let's think about the word *peacemaker* for a moment.

How to Be a Peacemaker

In my experience I have discovered that peace doesn't just occur in a family—you have to *make* it happen. After I became a follower of the Prince of Peace, I discovered that strange new desire had been born within me: the desire to be the peacemaker, when previously I had delighted in being the warmonger! How, then, do we go on to practice the heavenly art of "making" peace? Let's look at Nehemiah closely and find out.

It is encouraging to see that Nehemiah had some trouble controlling his own emotions. "When I heard their outcry and these charges, I was very angry," he says. But instead of blowing up in the situation and simply adding his own fallout to an already dangerous hot spot, he "pondered" these charges in his mind (5:7). The word *ponder* means to weigh and examine. In other words, Nehemiah carefully gathered the facts and looked at them in the sweet clarity of true impartiality, determining to calm down and see *both* sides of the problem. He gave himself time to think about the whole issue before he ever opened his mouth to judge it! Oh, that you and I would "ponder" rather than provoke or pontificate within due consideration. If only we would learn to "cool it" and thereby give ourselves time to examine the problem. If only we would wait until we could be objective rather than subjective, we might find ourselves being used by the Lord, as Nehemiah was used, to turn the whole thing to good. How, then, after exerting our will to ponder, do we proceed to mediate the crisis?

1. Be Accessible

First, Nehemiah was accessible. And I believe he had practiced this particular art for as long as God had allowed him to be around Jerusalem. In 4:21 we read: "So we continued the work." Then in chapter 5, we note that as governor he could say, "The earlier governors . . . lorded it over the people. But out of reverence for God I did not act like that" (v. 15). Yes, Nehemiah clearly *practiced* the art of being accessible.

Many people have practiced being *in*accessible to each other for so long that a great suspicion has taken root which sadly prevents them from being able to be of any help at all. If no one has been a patient bridger of communication gaps over the years, different family factions will spend their time yelling at each other across the well-dug chasms of misunderstanding, and when trouble comes, there will be no one available as a peacemaker who has won their confidence.

Practicing this art means beginning as soon as we are aware that we belong to a family. A child can be asked to be accessible to another child when geometry has to be mastered or help is needed with a difficult project. He can be trained to be helpful to his parents on weekends, as well as being taught to be an encouragement to his friends when they fall out with each other. Then we who are parents can practice this art of being reachable when our children are very small, particularly as we tuck them up into bed at night. We must discipline ourselves for that last and most important time of day, when a story or simply some tired chatter-time is a must. Bedtime is a marvelous opportunity to just "be there"; and yet often it is the time of day when parents are at their very worst—tired out, impatient to finish their duties and be free to do their own thing. If this is the case, our children will quickly sense that frustrated impatience and clam up on us, beginning a habit of concealing the information they would really like the opportunity to share. We cannot expect our teen-agers to suddenly start sharing their deepest struggles if we have never proved our attentive interest in their day-to-day ones!

My husband works at home. Having led a busy life traveling for long periods of time, he has had little opportunity to be around our children physically. When a change of schedule occurred, he chose to have his office at home so he could make up

for lost time. This involved obvious work hazards, but he made it
a rule that however busy he was, he would never close his study
door. He wanted to show the children he was well within reach
and that in no way were they to consider themselves "shut out"
by his work.

There are many practical ways of proving to people that we are
accessible. When children tumble off the bus and through the
kitchen door at the end of their day, do we greet them or are we
invariably on the phone, meeting them with a disappointing,
"Shhh! I'm talking!" We need to try limiting our phone conversations to a ten-minute period, at least when the kids are around;
and we should tell them we've done that because we want them
to know we are open to their needs. How many times does a
child say to us at bedtime, "Come up with me, mother"—and do
we? Or do we say impatiently, "Oh, go on. You're old enough to
put yourself to bed," which may be true, but means we've missed
the signal completely! The message that has been tentatively
extended toward us at that point has been "Please come with me
because I need you all to myself—and I need you *now*."

When Judy is home from college, she and I still enjoy that
special period together, even though she is now in her twenties.
It's been a matter of being accessible to her when *she's* asked for
it, not just when it coincided with *my* convenient schedule.
Cultivating the hearing habit has paid off marvelously. Many a
bedtime has been used as a bridge by both of us as we have
walked over our differences and taken each other's hand. So first,
if we would be a Nehemiah, we must practice "being there,"
however inconvenient it may prove to be.

2. Be Knowledgable

Second, we need to be knowledgable. If we are going to be a
"maker of peace," we will have to know certain things. What are
they? In chapter 5, we hear Nehemiah telling the offending party:

> What you are doing is not right. Shouldn't you walk in the fear of
> our God to avoid the reproach of our Gentile enemies? I and my
> brothers and my men are also lending the people money and

grain. But let the exacting of usury stop! Give back to them immediately their fields, vineyards, olive groves and houses, and also the usury you are charging them—the hundredth part of the money, grain, new wine and oil" (vv. 9-11).

When we are called on to preside over a conflict, we will have to develop judgment according to knowledge. Our family must be thoroughly familiar with certain principles upon which they are expected to act. We parents must determine what those principles are and make sure our children are clearly taught them, not left to guess what we expect of them. Nehemiah made his judgments concerning the "great outcry" according to the revealed will of God. *To be able to do that, we have to know what the Word of God says about the will of God.* For example, in the conflict in question, the problem of partiality had arisen. Nehemiah knew that God had commanded a reverence for the value of each individual and therefore was able to bring things to a happy conclusion.

I remember our two older children marching number-three child before me and accusing him of standing up for his rights! "Just who does he think he is?" demanded number one.

"Why, he suddenly has started to act as if he is as important as we are!" added number two indignantly.

"Well, of course he is," I replied. "You've never met an unimportant person! God says that every single human being is just as valuable as the next. Peter is just beginning to discover that everyone is number one in God's eyes, even if they are number three in the family pecking order!" I was able to tell our older children that obvious fact because we had based our family structure on scriptural principles, and because I knew the Word of God teaches the intrinsic value of the individual.

I believe that Nehemiah was knowledgable because he had cultivated a deep sense of accountability to the Lord and to the teaching of His principles on a daily practical level. He knew that the Book of Deuteronomy taught:

These commandments that I give you today are to be upon your hearts. Impress them on your children. Talk about them when you sit at home and when you walk along the road, when you lie down and when you get up. Tie them as symbols on your hands and bind them on your foreheads. Write them on the door-frames of your houses and on your gates (6:6-9).

3. Be Creative

But Nehemiah did more than make himself accessible to the warring factions within the city walls and be knowledgable concerning the godly principles he was called upon to teach. He demonstrated a creative ability in the execution of those beliefs. Refusing to follow the pattern of his predecessors who used their position of privilege to their own advantage, excluding people rather than inviting them to share their lives, he opened his home and worked at being hospitable!

> Moreover, from the twentieth year of King Artaxerxes, when I was appointed to be their governor in the land of Judah, until his thirty-second year—twelve years—neither I nor my brothers ate the foot allotted to the governor. But the earlier governors—those preceding me—placed a heavy burden on the people and took forty shekels of silver from them in addition to food and wine. Their assistants also lorded it over the people. But out of reverence for God I did not act like that. Instead, I devoted myself to the work on this wall. All my men were assembled there for the work; we did not acquire any land.

> Furthermore, a hundred and fifty Jews and officials ate at my table, as well as those who came to us from the surrounding nations. Each day one ox, six choice sheep and some poultry were prepared for me, and every ten days an abundant supply of wine of all kinds. In spite of all this, I never demanded the food allotted to the governor, because the demands were heavy on these people (Neh. 5:14-18).

Like Nehemiah, we have let our children know that we want our home to be a resource center for others. We have made it clear that it is as open to their friends as to ours. Sometimes, like Nehemiah, we have felt as though there were indeed 150 people at our table, but we have worked at being hospitable, sharing our blessings with those less fortunate than ourselves and letting the kids be part of that very special sharing. Consequently our children have been constantly exposed to families in the midst of terrible, tearing traumas and have witnessed the blessings of those brought to the Lord for His help and His healing. As a result, they have shared with us the desire to imitate the same ministering attitude should God gift them with their own homes and families someday.

Another thing we have learned to do as a family has been to work at being creatively thoughtful toward each other. For instance, we have busied ourselves thinking of ways of giving different members of the family *time* instead of *things*. One day we decided that birthdays and Christmas had become burdens, times of common dread. What a shame! The problem had arisen over the matter of giving and receiving gifts. What should we buy for one another that we did not already possess? we wondered. We came to the conclusion that one of the best presents we could possibly choose was time together, rather than just more things that we didn't need or even want. And so it became a habit to seek to be innovative and buy "events" for each other that would necessitate spending precious moments together. For example, Pete, who is a sports buff, bought basketball tickets for Dave (two of them, of course) so they could enjoy an evening watching their favorite sport. Stuart gave Judy and Dave seats for a repertory performance of *Romeo and Juliet*, which meant that brother and sister had to make the effort to get all dressed up and go off together for a special evening of entertainment. Judy gave Stuart and me dinner for two at a cozy and isolated restaurant (a rare opportunity that we would probably never have chosen for ourselves). And Dave gave Judy money for phone calls for some sister/brother communication during her freshman year of college! Other ideas followed: a weekend for Pete at Judy's college, a few hours court time at the racquetball club, an overnight for Stuart and me in a nearby hotel—just to get away from it all. Time—time for each other instead of things!

You will find that it's hard to get into a family row when your home is constantly overflowing with other people to whom you need to give time—people you all need to serve. You discover that you don't have too much energy left to fight each other when you are busy fighting for the blind, the halt, and the lame who have been welcomed to your table! It's also awfully hard to fall out with someone when opportunities for understanding have been regularly built into your busy schedule.

4. Be Prayerful

I don't think we can end this chapter without considering one more thing. It is the practice of being prayerful! There is no more effective weapon for Christians as they seek to resolve family conflicts than the weapon of prayer. Through intercession we can bring the Prince of Peace onto the scene of hostilities. There have been many times in the past when I have quietly left the "war" and retired behind the lines to plead for peace. There have been many occasions when I have fasted and prayed for one or another of our children who had fallen out with a brother or sister or one of us parents. I have discovered at such times that my own attitude has been changed, or I have received a clarity of insight into the situation, or I have been given a clear directive from God's Word that I have been able to act upon.

Prayer also links us with the Creator, the expert at originating original ideas. Maybe you are not a creative person yourself. Well, I have great news—He is! And not only that, He is ready and willing to impart to us all sorts of ideas about things to do together that we might develop happy and healthy relationships. So often it is a case of having not because we ask not!

So let us stand guard at the Horse Gate, so that carefully—and prayerfully—conflicts become opportunities for good instead of evil; so that home becomes a place of blessing instead of a place of cursing—a place of growth that can lead to a harmonious coexistence in the family that professes to honor the Lord, or even in the family that doesn't! And one more thing: Don't wail, "But it's so hard to be a Nehemiah when I'm the only Christian in our home." Begin to be the peacemaker our Prince of Peace calls you to be, and you won't be the only one for very long!

Worksheet

A. *Favoritism*
  1. Read Nehemiah 5:1-6.
     a. Have you ever been a victim of favoritism?
     b. As parents, why do you think we clash with our children at different stages of their development?
  2. Comment on the relevance of the following verses:
     a. A model: Romans 2:11; Deuteronomy 10:17-19.
     b. A command and warning: Ephesians 6:4; Colossians 3:21.
  3. Discuss the real-life situations from the following texts and note the long-range results of playing favorites (read all of the passages before discussion): Genesis 25:27; 27:41-42; 37:1-4, 19-28.
  4. It takes only one person's willingness to be different to stem the flow of evil and turn the situation into blessing.
     a. Read Genesis 50:15-27.
     b. Discuss Joseph's behavior, particularly in verse 20.
     c. If you had been in Joseph's sandals, what would you have done?

B. *Warmonger Or Peacemaker?*
  Whatever we have been in the past, we will need to change if we profess to belong to the Prince of Peace. The first step we will need to take is that of working at the art of being *accessible*.
  1. When a conflict arises in your family, how do you see yourself?
     judge   jury   accused   spectator
     prosecutor   counsel for the defense   recorder
     reporter   absent from court
  2. Nehemiah practiced the art of being accessible to people. How can we do the same? Is there a cost involved? Discuss.
  3. Note the beautiful example of our Lord Jesus Christ: Luke 6:17-19; 8:40-46.
     a. This did not mean He never experienced the pressures and frustrations of being constantly available (see Luke 9:37-41).
     b. But little prevented Him from being there when someone needed Him. Notice the variety of people Jesus was "there" for: Luke 4:16; 7:1ff., 36-38; 8:47; 9:38-39; 11:14, 37; 12:1; 13:10ff.; 15:1; 17:11-14; 18:35ff.; 19:1-5.

C. *Knowledge of God's Word*

1. To be able to minister in family conflict requires an ability to identify the source of the problem, the willingness to be available to God and to the people in need, and a knowledge of the Word of God concerning the will of God in the matter! We will find it difficult to act as arbiter if we do not have any knowledge of the basic biblical principles of human behavior.

2. Read Deuteronomy 6 aloud. Then answer the following questions:

   a. What was the point of Moses' teaching the children of Israel to observe God's laws, decrees, and commands (vv. 1-2)? (See also Deuteronomy 4:9; 5:31-33.)

   b. What is the promise given as an incentive to obedience (v. 3)? (See also Deuteronomy 11:18-21.)

   c. Where are God's words to find a home (v. 6)? Write out this verse in your own words. (See also Psalm 119:9, 11.)

   d. Under what circumstances do families tend to *forget* God's laws (vv. 10-12)?

   e. When our children ask us spiritual questions, why do we have no excuse as to what we shall say (vv. 20-25)?

D. *Resourcefulness*

   Discuss some practical ways of giving each other *time* instead of *things* for presents.

E. *Prayer*

1. Corporate prayer time: Pray about specific areas of conflict within your own family circle. (Be general and tactful.)

2. Personal prayer time: Spend time silently talking to the Lord about the things He has impressed on you in this lesson concerning *your* part in helping to resolve family conflicts.

7

The Dung Gate: Forgiveness

The Dung Gate was repaired by Malkijah son of Recab, ruler of the district of Beth Haccerem. He rebuilt it and put its doors and bolts and bars in place (Neh. 3:14).

The Dung Gate was the place where the dirt was dealt with. Jerusalem did not sweep its rubbish into corners or rearrange it neatly into piles. Knowing the potential health hazards of heaps of refuse, the inhabitants simply removed them through the Dung gate to prevent the spread of disease. In the same way, there has to be a place where the dirt is dealt with in our lives. Garbage that is pushed into the corners of our minds or rearranged and left for future disposal will most surely be trouble's breeding ground. In this chapter we shall be talking about such things as sin, guilt, and forgiveness. The dirt represents the sin we commit; guilt is its festering product; and forgiveness is the only broom that can sweep it all out of the city gates.

Practicing Forgiveness

Someone has said, "A good marriage is made up of two good forgivers." A healthy family certainly provides the opportunity to practice forgiveness, enabling us to form the habit early in life. Hopefully this will prevent us from ending up living in a house full of strangers.

We begin our practice as children, forgiving our mothers for forcing us to eat all the things that are "good for us" (which usually means the food that tastes awful!). We may have to forgive our harried and harassed parents for not showing the appropriate appreciation of our grandest efforts or for drawing unfair and unwelcome attention to our greatest failures. We will undoubtedly need to forgive our guardians for laying protective rules on us, restrictions that simply reflect their hidden anxiety for our well-being. Sadly, some of us will have memories of downright abuse to deal with, while others will struggle with the scars of neglect or just plain bad parenting.

Yes, the family is a marvelous place to practice the art of forgiveness. If we get married, we will need to forgive our partners for all the habits that irritate us when viewed "up close." There may be big problems, disclosed only after marriage, that need our attention; or there may be small concerns like the little foxes we read about in the Song of Songs that got among the vines and spoiled the fruit. They will have to be forgiven, too. The little fox of some irritating lifelong habit may appear to shatter our honeymoon joy—such as squeezing the toothpaste tube from the top rather than winding it up tidily (as it should be done, of course, because that's how *I've* always done it) from the bottom! There could be the little fox of casual, take-you-for-granted-now-that-we-are-married attitudes, or we may have to catch the little fox of bad communication.

Then when the babies appear on the scene, we will probably find it necessary to start practicing forgiveness all over again, on quite a different level. We will need to forgive our infants for being so insatiably hungry all the time and for waking us up with such insistent and monotonous regularity every night. I don't believe there are too many mothers who jump up and down for joy at the prospect of yet one more interrupted night's sleep!

I well remember being at the end of my tether, struggling to keep my eyes open through yet one more interminable night feeding and finding that it was very hard to forgive my own baby for being so horribly inconsiderate! Hard on the heels of that challenge came the next, that of forgiving my husband for his somnambulant posture and his happy snores as he dreamt his way through the whole thing!

One night the very force of my baleful glare must have permeated his subconscious slumber because he woke up and sleepily muttered, "What—what are you doing, dear?"

"I'm busy murdering your child!" I snapped angrily.

"Good—good—that's very good," he murmured, happily returning to sleep. The broom of forgiveness was very busy in our early married years!

It was very hard for me as a young and seemingly permanently tired mother of three preschoolers not to expect a lot of help from my husband, a lending hand to lighten my load. When he didn't always come through with it, I needed to forgive him. Resentments and misunderstandings can flourish in those sorts of situations, so Stuart and I worked out a basic principle then that we have sought to practice ever since—that of obeying the scriptural injunction not to allow "the sun to go down on our anger." Whatever anger or hurt had been inflicted on the other during the day, we promised to resolve it before we retired that night, thus keeping short accounts with each other. It was one of the best habits we could establish. For if hot anger solidifies, it settles into cold hostility, which can become a sharp and terrible nail in the coffin of any relationship!

When your children are small, you will have a grand opportunity to practice forgiving your toddler for being a "terrible two," and then a worse three, and after that an unbelievable four! As your youngsters race toward maturity, you will most certainly have to forgive them for being thirteen! There will be many a bitter word, cruel action, and rude response as well as hurt feelings to cope with—yes, sticky situations ad infinitum will surely arise in any normal family circle, between mother-in-law and daughter-in-law, son-in-law and everything-else-in-law. Even our own aging parents may well have catalogs of real or imagined offenses stored away in their memories and all the time in the world to live them out again and again. A "good" family is the one that is committed to forgive each other on an ongoing basis, for forgiveness truly takes a commitment like that. It is a choice, a deliberate decision that begins in the mind, usually as a response to an explanation of the Christian gospel. The Good News of our own pardon by the Great Forgiver needs to form the whole basis of our relationship with Him and with others.

Why Forgiveness?

But what is the cause of all this need for forgiveness? In other words, what makes people do the things that others have to forgive? To put it bluntly, the Scriptures tell us that we live in a sick world as sick people born to a sick society; and quite frankly, sick folks do not generally make for easy relationships and good company! I am not, of course, talking about a physical ailment, but rather a spiritual malady—that of sin sickness!

God's Word tells us that sin is the root cause of this universal problem that produced actions that need to be forgiven. Sin is a coming short of God's standard, which is a demonstration of the Christlike life. In other words, sin is being un-Christlike. Maybe you have an uncommon aversion to the word *sin,* so let us use another word. How about *trespass?* Trespass means to willfully step over the line—with a flagrant disregard for the rules, which in this case have been drawn up for us by the Rule-maker and which we call the Ten Commandments. *Guile* is yet another word describing the "dirt" that litters the "inner city" of our hearts. Guile means the capacity we all have to pervert or twist that which is good into a tangled travesty of the original—for example, the way we so often and easily turn loving into lusting.

If we think of all this in relation to our families, then we can see how sin is the cause of all the trouble. Was there ever a time in your childhood when you were less than Christlike? What about your obligations to your husband or your wife or your parents? Have you ever "stepped over the line" and not played by the rules of fairness and decency where your children are concerned? What about perverting that which is good or just generally coming short of the standard that God requires of you in your dealings with your family? If we are honest, we all have to admit that we have done some or all of these things, and there is undoubtedly dirt in our lives—dirt that must have greatly offended a clean and holy-minded God. Maybe it is time to be sorry enough about it all that we meet Him at the Dung Gate and repent!

Source of Forgiveness

If the cause of all the trouble is sin and selfishness, the source of all our forgiveness is God Himself. I do not believe we can truly learn to forgive other people until we have come to a personal realization of what it means to be forgiven. We have all sinned against God, for any sin against man is a sin against God. We tend to strut around our world in unbelievable arrogance, saying proudly and belligerently, "I forgive me." But you can't forgive your own sin—the One you have offended has to do that!

There was once a woman who was a sinner. She appeared at a meal that Jesus and a rich Pharisee were having together and began to act in a seemingly distraught way—washing the Lord's feet with tears of repentence and drying them with her hair. The Lord, discerning the Pharisee's critical attitude toward her, commented on the fact that the woman whose sins were indeed many had been forgiven and that was why she was publicly demonstrating her love with such abandon. "She who is forgiven much," Jesus explained, "loves much! Correspondingly, he or she who thinks they are forgiven little will love little!" Among the many lessons in this beautiful little incident in the Gospels lies an important factor regarding the whole matter of forgiveness. Forgiveness is intrinsically bound up with love! Love—true love—forgives anything, even the hands that crucify it. As we get a picture of the love of God in Christ upon the cross, then we get a glimpse of the size of our forgiveness. We then "love because He first loved us" (1 John 4:19).

But just how much has God had to forgive? Think about it for a moment. You and I may struggle with one or two people who have hurt us. Maybe some of us have a whole score of folk who have wounded us. But even if we feel the whole world is against us, in our saner moments we would have to admit that this just cannot be true, because we don't know the whole world, and the whole world does not know us! Even the whole city we live in is hardly aware of our existence. In fact, we may have to admit that not everyone on our own street knows our name! Our circle of acquaintances is really miniscule when we get it all into perspective. But for God it is a different matter. The Bible tells us that every human being who has ever been or ever will be is known, and known to have offended Him. He has sin to pardon in every single man, woman, and child—in every country in every age.

Let's take this a step further. We usually think we *know* what it is we need to forgive people for. But this is not always true either. The offense may have seemed to us a very blatant, black-and-white situation; but just imagine how many factors we cannot possibly be aware of—motives and reasons for people's words or actions for example. Perhaps I think someone should be saying he is sorry to me when it is *I* who should be doing that! And then there are all the nasty things people have said to others about us or thought about us that we never even find out about. These are things we should forgive them for, too! But if we don't know about them, how can we? you ask. In fact you are probably glad that you don't know because you're having enough trouble trying to forgive people for the things you *do* know about!

But can you imagine what it is like for God? He knows it all! The Bible teaches us that there is no thought or action hidden from Him. Even the intentions of a person's heart—which may not see the light of day in actions because they simply lack the opportunity to be born in some form of malevolent behavior—are fully felt by the omniscient God, as if they have indeed already been perpetrated. Somewhere in the sphere of eternity God had to face the problem of what to do with all that dirt!

I love the Lord for the way He handled His problem. How

much I can learn from Him! He never simply snaps His fingers so that His problems disappear (although He most certainly has all the power necessary to take that course of action if He so desires). I know He doesn't do that because, if He did, *we* would all disappear, for we *are* His problems! God had to decide just what He was going to do with a human race who had broken His rules.

The problem must have been compounded because He was not duty-bound to solve it. He didn't owe us anything. He was and is "free" of all His obligations toward mankind. We have sinned so dreadfully that we deserve only His judgment and oblivion. Think of how many sins are represented by the entire human race! Not only sins of commission, but sins of omission as well. As the creed says, "We have done those things which we ought not to have done, and we have not done those things that we ought to have done, and there is no health in us." No wonder the cry comes from the hearts of those of us who fully recognize the immensity of our sin and therefore the size of our forgiveness: "Have mercy on us miserable offenders!" In the midst of much lamentation Jeremiah the prophet bursts out with the words, "Because of the LORD's great love we are not consumed, for his compassions never fail. They are new every morning; great is your faithfulness" (Lam. 3:22-23).

So God in His freedom made an eternal decision from the basis of His agape love: He decided to deal with the dirt and offer us forgiveness. Being a just Judge, He knew He would have to find a willing substitute who would bear His wrath against sin in our place, and Jesus was willing! To put it another way, God chose not to forgive Jesus so that He might forgive us! His justice was satisfied, for a holy God must punish sin, but His love for us could be manifested, not only by Christ's death on the cross, but by the offer of divine forgiveness because of it. Agape love has told us in actions and words that forgiveness is indeed available, but we need to realize that it is only ours for the taking because He has punished the sinner in Christ. Forgiveness is ours because He swept, through Christ's death, all that sin away with the broom of His judgment. That same broom can now become an instrument of blessing and cleansing, sweeping our lives free from all our offenses against Him and against others.

If you ever get around to telling God that you are sorry for the grief you have caused Him, you will find that it will begin to be easier to say you are sorry to other people for the grief you have caused them; and as you make a practice of an attitude of gratitude, you will even begin to find that it becomes possible to forgive others for the grief they have caused you! It is for this reason I say that we cannot start to forgive others until we have some idea of the cost to God of our own redemption. The sinful woman had been forgiven much. She knew it! She had been loved much, and she knew that too! Her heart response was to love in return.

Christians are commanded to demonstrate an attitude of forgiveness toward their persecutors. This will mark them as Christ's men and women, for did not Jesus pray to the rhythm of the hammer, "Father, forgive them, for they know not what they do"? While the angry mob was stoning Stephen, we are told that he followed His Master's example by asking as he died that the Lord Jesus would receive his spirit—and that he would not hold this sin against his murderers. Stephen, I think you will admit, had much to forgive, but then he knew that he'd been forgiven much more. When that's the case, it makes it easier to pray such prayers.

Christians forgive. Paul and Silas forgave the Philippian jailer for fastening them in the cruel stocks. There was no hint of vengeance in evidence when God sent His angel to open the prison doors. We read that when the Philippian jailer saw that the prison doors had been opened, he drew his sword and was about to kill himself because he thought his prisoners had escaped. But Paul shouted to him, "Don't harm yourself—we're all here." Paul didn't have to shout—he could have remained silent. In fact, it must have been tempting to let the man go ahead and kill himself; after all, Paul and Silas must have suffered at his hand. But, you see, Paul counted himself chief of sinners, and so he had little trouble forgiving any other sinner of lesser rank.

Christians forgive because God can deal with our bitter, sick spirits and mend them into mobility so they can reach out in reconciliation.

What and Who to Forgive

Now let us consider *what* God expects us to forgive. There are some instances of man's inhumanity to man that defy imagination. We reason that God will surely understand if the woman who is raped is unable to forgive her attacker, or if the wife who has watched helplessly as another woman has stolen her husband's heart away cannot forgive the thief. And what about the mother who sees her son destroyed by the drug pusher and quite understandably detests the spoiler of her child? Surely God understands if we do not pardon *these* things. In other words, we tend to believe that some things are forgivable and others are not.

When Jesus said, "Forgive, and you will be forgiven" (Luke 6:37c), He was looking into the faces of twelve men whom He knew with certainty would have much to forgive before they arrived safely home in heaven. He knew that Peter would be martyred. That John would spend his old age on the Isle of Patmos incarcerated in an underground quarry. All, except Judas, would suffer for their faith. Yet Jesus called them and us to forgive "whatever"—with apparently no exceptions. The answer to the question, *"what* do we forgive?" appears to be—*everything.*

Consider the account of Corrie ten Boom's postwar meeting with the prison officer who had been particularly cruel to her sister in the concentration camp in which they were held during World War II.

> It was at a church service in Munich that I saw him, the former S.S. man who had stood guard at the shower room door in the processing center at Ravensbruck. He was the first of our actual jailers that I had seen since that time. And suddenly it was all there—the roomful of mocking men, the heaps of clothing, Betsie's pain-blanched face.

He came up to me as the church was emptying, beaming, and bowing. "How grateful I am for your message, Fraulein," he said. "To think that, as you say, He has washed my sins away!"

His hand was thrust out to shake mine. And I, who had preached so often to the people in Bloemendaal the need to forgive, kept my hand at my side.

Even as the angry, vengeful thoughts boiled through me, I saw the sin of them. Jesus Christ had died for this man; was I going to ask for more? Lord Jesus, I prayed, forgive me and help me to forgive him.

I tried to smile, I struggled to raise my hand. I could not. I felt nothing, not the slightest spark of warmth or charity. And so again I breathed a silent prayer. Jesus, I cannot forgive him. Give me Your forgiveness.

As I took his hand the most incredible thing happened. From my shoulder along my arm and through my hand a current seemed to pass from me to him, while into my heart sprang a love for this stranger that almost overwhelmed me.

And so I discovered that it is not on our forgiveness any more than on our goodness that the world's healing hinges, but on His. When He tells us to love our enemies, He gives, along with the command, the love itself.[1]

So we do have dramatic modern examples to inspire us. But we also need to look closer to home and realize that it is often just as hard to forgive our families for some apparently small thing as it is for us to forgive strangers for the big things. God expects us to forgive everything *everybody* does! We must forgive our friends, our enemies, and our relatives, too. That will distinguish us from those who have not been forgiven by God. In Luke 6:32ff. Jesus says that even sinners do quite well where relationships with their "own" are concerned, but they don't do nearly such a good job with people who are not like themselves. Christians, He said, have to do better than that! We have to forgive people who are not like us for not being like us! We have to forgive everybody. We even have to forgive ourselves.

One problem we all have to face is guilt. Remember, if rubbish is left, it festers—and that is a pretty accurate picture of guilt! The only way I know of coping with guilt is to realize that God's forgiveness adequately deals with it. He tells us He has cast all our sins into the depths of the sea and has put up a NO FISHING sign. The problem some of us have is that we insist on fishing up that which has been cast into the depths of God's sea of forgiveness. Guilt is fishing! God has told us that "[our] sins and lawless acts [He] will remember no more" (Heb. 10:17), and yet we insist on remembering what He has insisted on forgetting! We have to confess our sins to God, believe in faith He has heard and forgiven us and cleansed us from all unrighteousness, and then forgive ourselves. Think of it! What God has cast from us we have no business retrieving, and what God has forgiven we have no right to remember! We must forgive ourselves. Have you been liberated from guilt? Mother guilt, wife guilt, daughter-in-law guilt, husband guilt? So when we ask ourselves *who* must we forgive, the answer is *everybody*. Not everybody except her or him or myself—but *everybody*, meaning *everybody*!

When to Forgive

Does God expect us to forgive the same offense over and over again? The answer is yes! Apparently God does not keep count of how many times He has to forgive *us* for committing the "same old sin." I once heard of an African tribe who had a very simple way of counting: one, two, three, a lot! I believe that's the way God counts, too. We read in the Word that God deals in "multitudes" of sins. That's why one day Jesus answered Peter's question "How many times shall I forgive my brother when he sins against me? Up to seven times?" by telling him, "I tell you, not seven times, but seventy-seven times" (Matt. 18:21-22). This was a colloquial phrase meaning ad infinitum—or one, two, three, a lot. In other words, love doesn't keep count! Forgiveness isn't very good at arithmetic. It has never learned how. So, *When* should I forgive? very simple: *every time*.

How to Forgive

Finally, we need to ask, *how* do I forgive? The answer to that question has already been given in part. We forgive as God in

Christ has forgiven us. We have our model, and we should refresh our minds as to how He does it and then seek to imitate Him. Just how *does* He do it?

First of all, God forgives us *freely*. There are absolutely no strings attached. He doesn't make us pay for it. He knows we do not have enough currency to do so anyway, so He doesn't bother asking. We are not to make others pay for their offenses toward us either. We are to forgive *freely*. Forgiveness is priceless and therefore cannot be bought—it has to be given.

Second, God forgives us *fully*. When we apply this, it means we won't nag or carefully keep a record of the wrong done to us so we can remind the one who has wounded us of it. When we have been hurt, it is all too easy to wait till the next round in the ring and then produce a punch we've been saving just in case we got the chance to deliver it! *Fully* means *fully*. It means we forgive it all, not half of it; and we forgive from the heart. The proof that we have been able to do this will be evidenced by the fact that we don't nag. Nagging is unforgiveness demanding to be heard. It is also terribly hard to live with. Beware of it! As the Book of Proverbs tells us, "A quarrelsome wife is like a constant dripping on a rainy day . . ." (27:15). Nagging is like a constant dripping! In some countries they torture people like that! God doesn't nag us about what we have done because He has forgiven us *fully*. Nagging reminds us of things that are being carefully remembered, and that brings me to the third point.

God forgives us *forgetfully!* To forgive and forget is important, and only God can help us with this one. Charles Swindoll, spoke of this on a radio program, saying: "Those who choose not to forget remain tied to the past. Those who forgive and forget, can move ahead to new areas. Forgetting enables me not to be petty and negative. Forgetting frees me to live for tomorrow rather than being anchored to yesterday!"

I am sure there are some things we will never be able to forget until we get to heaven and are "like Him." But we can help ourselves not to dwell on them, refusing to turn the "re-runs" on in our minds. We can do what the apostle Paul instructs us to do and "take captive every thought to make it obedient to Christ" (2 Cor. 10:5)—in other words, put a noose around its neck and lead it to Jesus to let Him deal with it. And then we can pray for the person who has wronged us. It is amazing how prayer changes attitudes and heals bad memories.

Will You Forgive?

Lastly, some of us will have to forgive—not only our families or our relatives, not only our neighbors or our enemies or even ourselves—some of us will have to forgive God! As He has sought to bring us to Himself, we have often resisted Him and landed in serious trouble. Then we have blamed Him for the consequences of our own folly! Remember, He will always allow us to live with the results of our own stupidity. Chapter 9 of the Book of Nehemiah gives us a full account of the confession of the Israelites. Looking back over a long history of hard-hearted pride and arrogance, they were able to say, "But you are a forgiving God, gracious and compassionate, slow to anger and abounding in love. . . . In all that has happened to us, you have been just; you have acted faithfully, while we did wrong" (vv. 17b, 33).

The Bible says, "The goodness of God leads us to repentance"; and if we, like those Israelites of Nehemiah's day, would not remind ourselves of God's care and compassion, then perhaps we too would see that if "we are slaves today," it is because of *our* wrongdoing, not *His!* Maybe we need to forgive God for something He hasn't even done!

So my challenge to you is this: *Will* you forgive? Please notice that I didn't say, *Can* you? but *Will* you? If forgiveness is a command, then it is addressed to our wills and not to our emotions, and we need to kneel down and say first to God, "I will forgive" and then go by letter, phone, or in person and say the same thing to the one who has wronged us.

Then, *what* do you forgive? Everything. *Who* do you forgive? Everybody. *When* do you forgive? one, two, three, a lot! *How* do you forgive? Like God—freely, fully, and forgetfully.

Will you forgive? is a question only *you* can answer!

Forgiveness, who had just been born of Grace, looked around for
someone to forgive.
"What shall we call him?" asked Grace of the Father.
"I like Forgiveness myself," said God.
"Why, I would never have thought of calling him that!" said
Grace.
"It means 'sending away,'" said God.
"Oh," said Grace, a little bewildered.
"Is that what he will be doing? Sending away?"
"Yes," said the Father simply.
Forgiveness grew up, and when he was old enough, the Father told him
it was time to leave home.
"I'm going with you," said the Son.
Forgiveness was delighted.
"I'll need your help down there," said Jesus softly, pointing to our
world.
Forgiveness had developed a beautiful body. Strong and straight. He
was almost proud of his muscles, but no one was really proud of
anything in heaven, so he was content to look at all those rippling
sinews and wonder why the Father had had him work out so long on
the heavenly weights. But once he was in our world it didn't take him
long to understand why. What an awful lot of strength was needed
to forgive!
"I want you to live with Mary and Joseph while I'm growing up,"
said Jesus. "They will be needing you."
Sure enough, before long forgiveness was needed because Herod tried
to kill their baby.
Then when Jesus stayed behind in Jerusalem to talk to the learned
men, he needed to help Mary to forgive Jesus
for being twelve.
When Jesus was thirty, it was time for Him to begin
His ministry.
There was so much work that Forgiveness fell into bed at night,
too exhausted to do anything but dream of heaven!
Jesus used him all the time—but he had to admit it was
nice to be needed!

Jesus forgave His friends and He forgave His enemies.
　　He forgave the unbelief of His own family
　　　and the adultery of the woman.
He forgave the indifference of His disciples and
　　the doubts of His friends.
　　　He forgave the bickering of some
　　　　and the power plays of others.
He forgave the man with the nails and the hammer
　　and the ones who stripped Him naked too.
　　　He forgave those who railed on Him
and the one who put all His bones out of joint with the thrust of
　　the cross in the earth.
But only those who would accept Forgiveness were
　　allowed to come home with Him to heaven.
That made Forgiveness feel very important!
　　　But then of course He is! Nearly as important as
　　　　the One who made Him possible—
　　　　　Jesus Christ our Savior!

Notes

[1]Corrie ten Boom, The Hiding Place (Old Tappan, N.J.: Fleming H. Revell, 1971), p. 215.

Worksheet

A. *Dealing with the dirt: forgiveness*
  1. Discuss the things the Dung Gate can represent to us.
     a. God is our Role Model. Review 2 Corinthians 5:19. He alone can forgive sin (Mark 2:7; Ps. 86:5).
     b. God forgives us freely, fully, and forgetfully! Which of these aspects of forgiveness do you find hard to cope with where forgiving others is concerned?
  2. Look up and discuss the following verses:
     a. The *causes* for forgiveness: Luke 7:40-41; Colossians 3:13
     b. The *condition* of forgiveness: Matthew 6:12-15; 18:35; Luke 6:37
     c. The *constancy* of forgiveness: Matthew 18:21-22
  3. Our thoughts, from which evil actions spring, also need forgiveness. Read Acts 8:20-24.
     a. We need to confess our sin to Him and receive His promise (1 John 1:9).
     b. This will lead to
        (1) Happiness, the well-being of the soul (Ps. 32:1)
        (2) Healing of relationships (Eph. 4:32)
  4. Love is always slow to expose. It doesn't nag or gossip.
     a. Look up Proverbs 17:9; 27:15; James 1:26; 4:11
     b. What are some of the ways we might gossip or rejoice in iniquity in the name of Christ in a church situation?
  5. Discuss the statements "Love doesn't keep score" and "Nagging is unforgiveness demanding to be heard."

B. *Lessons on forgiveness from Nehemiah.*
  Read Nehemiah 9 and answer the following questions.
  1. In verses 7-8 we read about Abram. Think of the things Abram may have been tempted to blame God for. If you had been Abraham, who else would you have had a struggle to forgive? What was God's testimony to this man (v. 8)?
  2. In verses 9-12 we read about Egypt. Who took revenge on the Egyptians? What can we learn from this? Look up Romans 12:19.
  3. In verses 13-31 we have a catalog of the sins of God's people. Make a list of them. Put opposite each one the verse that has to do with God's antidote, forgiveness. For example, see the following page:

The Israelites' Sin	*God's Grace and Forgiveness*
disobeyed Law (v. 16)	God didn't desert them (v. 17)

4. Write out verse 33. This teaches us that we must never blame God if we have been deliberately willful.
5. Read 10:28-37 together and discuss the results of forgiveness.

C. *Prayer Time*
   1. Present your bodies and minds to God.
   2. Pray that He will enable you to practice a constant mind-set of love.
   3. Pray about anything that God has said to you from the study of Nehemiah 9.
   4. In silent prayer forgive others as He has forgiven you. That is, *freely, fully, forgetfully! Forever!*

8

The Valley Gate: Priorities

By night I went out through the Valley Gate toward the Jackal Well and the Dung Gate, examining the walls of Jerusalem, which had been broken down, and its gates, which had been destroyed by fire (Neh. 2:13).

If arguments arise in our family because someone is constantly creating or provoking hostility, it could well be because we do not know each other very well, and we need to ask ourselves what preventative steps we can take to minimize the cause of conflict. If we are regularly misjudging each other's attitudes and actions, then perhaps we need to learn how to communicate with each other. Hopefully, then we will not need to practice forgiveness on such a discouragingly regular basis.

One aspect of communication is the verbal explanation of ourselves and our behavior to those closest to us. But if we would enjoy such personal explanations, we must recognize the necessity of taking time to do it. Let's be more specific and practical. If we could get a handle on time management, for instance, we would find the space to do the things we know we should do instead of just dreaming about doing them. Involved in time management is the whole subject of *establishing priorities*, and the Valley Gate can give us a graphic illustration of this subject.

The Valley of Ben Hinnom

Outside the Valley Gate lay the Valley of Ben Hinnom. This was the place where kings Ahaz and Manasseh had perpetrated dastardly, idolatrous practices. Both of these leaders of Israel had had a godly heritage, but in 2 Chronicles we read that Ahaz,

> unlike David his father, . . . did not do what was right in the eyes of the LORD. He walked in the ways of the kings of Israel and also made cast idols for worshiping the Baals. He burned sacrifices in the Valley of Ben Hinnom and sacrificed his sons in the fire, following the detestable ways of the nations the LORD had driven out before the Israelites. He offered sacrifices and burned incense at the high places, on the hilltops and under every spreading tree (28:1a-4).

Likewise, Manasseh

> did evil in the eyes of the LORD, following the detestable practices of the nations the LORD had driven out before the Israelites. He rebuilt the high places his father Hezekiah had demolished; he also erected altars to the Baals and made Asherah poles. He bowed down to all the starry hosts and worshiped them. He built altars in the temple of the LORD, of which the LORD had said, "My Name will remain in Jerusalem forever." He sacrificed his sons in the fire in the Valley of Ben Hinnom, practiced sorcery, divination and witchcraft, and consulted mediums and spiritists. He did much evil in the eyes of the LORD, provoking him to anger (33:2-6).

The Valley of Ben Hinnom was the site of the worst heathen practice of all—sacrificing human beings to Baal. And not only human beings, but children; and not only children, but (in Ahaz and Manasseh's case) their own sons! No wonder the Lord was "provoked to anger"!

It was not until eighteen-year-old King Josiah began to reign in Jerusalem that reforms were instituted throughout Israel and he pulled down the altars the kings of Judah had erected on the roof near the upper room of Ahaz, and the altars Manasseh had built in the two courts of the temple of the LORD. He removed them from there, smashed them to pieces and threw the rubble into the Kidron Valley. The king also desecrated the high places that were east of Jerusalem on the south of the Hill of Corruption—the ones Solomon king of Israel had built for Ashtoreth the vile goddess of the Sidonians, for Chemosh the vile god of Moab, and for Molech the detestable god of the people of Ammon. Josiah smashed the sacred stones and cut down the Asherah poles and covered the sites with human bones (vv. 12-14).

Most importantly, Josiah "desecrated Topheth, which was in the Valley of Ben Hinnom, so that no one could use it to sacrifice children in the fire to Molech" (v. 10). In other words, he dealt with the traditional place where the children were sacrificed. He removed it! Then he instituted reforms that would ensure that these terrible things would never happen again.

The whole story gives us a vivid picture of the problem we have in our present society. As we live our lives in our own generation (like the Israelite kings in their day), we find ourselves absorbing many of the idolatrous practices around us. We can see situations in which couples are sacrificing their marriages and parents are sacrificing their children. As the walls fall down around our families, it is often the children who suffer most. We can see how badly reforms are needed that will prevent its happening over and over again. In other words, we long for someone to deal with the awful practices going on in the Valley of Ben Hinnom. But this detestable disintegration doesn't happen overnight; and if we take a good straight look at our priorities, we may yet have time to institute some saving reforms.

Stop the Sacrifice

First of all, we need to stand still long enough to notice what is happening to our relationships. We have to slow down, look, and listen. We are back to Nehemiah's careful walk around the city of Jerusalem, surveying the damage. I have a little prayer on my desk, a prayer I am often too convicted to read!

> *Slow me down, Lord,*
> *I'm going too fast.*
> *I can't see my brother*
> *When he's walking past.*

Quite honestly, I have to admit that most days I don't even have *time* to read it! I know how hard it is to slow down, and I also know how easy it is—especially in Christian work—to run so fast and so hard for so long that you meet yourself coming back. If you're not careful, it's quite possible to run around till you are quite run down. You find yourself running out of running power, and yet you finish up running over everyone around you—especially your own family. Now this I can really speak to!

Not long ago I was sitting in church on a Sunday evening, thoroughly excited about the fact that all I was required to do at that moment in time was to *sit* in church! For one whole hour I was not expected to *do* anything—except listen, of course! I was intrigued by the text of the preacher. He was explaining something new and interesting from an obscure passage of Scripture. As he passed on to other things, I stayed with the text, arrested internally by my heavenly Policeman, who knew full well I had been breaking the speed limit for quite a spell! He knew I would have to take the consequences if I continued offering Christian service on such a scale. Not only would I find myself reaping the damaging results of my manifold activities, but my family would be "sacrificed" at that particular place.

The text told of the two sons of Aaron, Nadab and Abihu, who offered "unauthorized fire before the LORD, contrary to his command. So fire came out from the presence of the LORD and consumed them, and they died before the LORD" (Lev. 10:1-2). This lesser known Scripture spoke directly to my situation and prompted me to ask myself if the service I was so busily offering was authorized or not. Were the meetings I was taking, the books I was writing, the committee work in which I was engaged authorized or unauthorized by Him? I got the point of the story to my dilemma. If I was engaging in unauthorized service, as Nadab and Abihu, I was running the risk of being destroyed by the very ministry that I offered. The problem I faced was how to know which of the many opportunities given to me were authorized?

I thought of Jesus. He always seemed to know what to do. He said, "I have brought you glory on earth by completing the work you gave *me* to do" (John 17:4). He didn't finish anyone else's work; He finished *His own!* His *authorized* work. One day after facing a multitude of sick and dying people (in fact, the Bible says, "The whole town gathered at the door"), He spent time in prayer. Then He said to His disciples, "Let us go somewhere else—to the nearby villages—so I can preach there also. That is why I have come" (Mark 1:38). He apparently had no problem whatever discerning which work was authorized and which unauthorized! However, He was God.

But I am Jill, and I have discovered that it's not easy for me at all! There has to come a point, however, when I stop still long enough to ask myself the hard questions: Am I, in fact, being burned up or burned out by the service that I am ever-so-earnestly offering? If so, it may well be because I am in all sincerity offering unauthorized fire! At this point, I have to go out the Valley Gate and force myself to look into the Valley of Ben Hinnom and see if I am sacrificing anyone there—"There" being a schedule full of good, even spiritual, but not necessarily *authorized* activity!

It was at such a place that our eldest son arrested my attention one day and told me of a few things concerning our daughter Judy that I had been far too busy to notice. She was twelve at the time and was "on tiptoe ready to go"! I had to institute some reforms by canceling some meetings and establishing priorities afresh, making mother-and-daughter time a *must, not a maybe,* and thereby taking away the place of sacrifice.

Many a husband has been told by his wife that he is sacrificing his son because of his work or play schedule, and he just won't believe he is. One reason he doesn't believe it is that whenever he is around, the child behaves normally. I understand this very well. In the days when Stuart traveled so extensively, our older two children would show signs of "father hunger" as soon as he left for a three-month trip. Judy would start to sleepwalk the night he went away but would stop the night he returned. David would dig himself into a trench of truculent tantrums and begin to blank out on his schoolwork. Yet as soon as daddy was around again, they would be totally different children. How, then, could my husband possibly be expected to take me seriously when the family was so different when he was around? It was hard for him to reorganize his priorities when the "evidence" was to the contrary. As other facts emerged, however, such as bad report cards and various signs of inner distress, he took time out to institute reforms.

Reforms are never easy. For us in that instance it meant selling all that we owned and emigrating to a new country and culture. It involved leaving our relatives, friends, and a work that we loved and knew we could do for a new and untried ministry we didn't know if we'd even like and certainly did not know we could accomplish! But our children, especially David, knew that we had moved 3,000 miles so that the place of sacrifice could be removed and we might have the chance to grow as a family again. Knowing that he was the top priority, David's heart was healed, and things were turned completely around for all of us.

How Do We Stop?

Priorities change as we mature. Time is given here and can be withdrawn there. A child needs things today that he will not require tomorrow and vice versa. Today he needs a mother, tomorrow a brother, the next day a grandparent, and perhaps another time some personal quietude. So there is no set formula that anyone can offer because people are not mathematical problems; they are complex entities who are developing continually.

What we *do* need are some principles on which to base our priorities and the grace of God to enable us to be flexible as our relationships develop. Undoubtedly the first thing we need to do is make a decision that we will indeed establish priorities throughout our lives. Next we must promise our mates that we will watch out for the place of sacrifice and do all in our power to institute the necessary reforms to redress the situation.

One of the award-winning films of 1980 was *Kramer vs. Kramer*, the story of a marriage that was sacrificed because of a father's misplaced priorities. Though he identified the place of sacrifice as preoccupation with his business and instituted some hasty reforms, he was too late to save his marriage. He was however, in time to salvage his relationship with his son. One point that came across loud and clear in that movie was that the father had not been able to recognize the sign that would have told him the strain was becoming unbearable.

I thank God for a husband who so thoroughly understands me that he has known when to take the pressure off. Keeping one eye on my hectic activities, he occasionally stretches out a big hand, sits me down on his knee, and says, "Jill, the family has noticed that you are falling apart and fast disappearing from sight. What is happening?" In response I blurted out all the assignments that I have taken on—and on—and on!

Patiently he takes a note pad and tells me to list all the things to which I have committed myself. Then he helps me reorganize them as best I can in order of importance. This is harder, and sometimes we need to talk about it, as he sees things from a different perspective. Taking a good look at me and then a good long look at the list, he proceeds to strike out the bottom four items. "I think you can manage these three commitments," he will say. "That seems to be a reasonable and realistic load for you. But these last four, though they are important, are not as important as the others and certainly not more important than your health and our well-being! So let's see what we can do to extract you from those particular obligations!" The place of sacrifice has been identified, priorities have been reorganized, and reforms have been instituted. On what basis? First, on the basis of what is most important, and then on the basis of my husband's thorough knowledge of my abilities, strengths, and weaknesses. You may ask, then, what should be the *most* important thing in our lives? The answer to that is that God and His kingdom *must be* our top priority, but we need to help each other determine when to leave the pressure on and when to take the pressure off, as we seek to accomplish that goal.

A friend of mine started work in a real-estate business because she wanted to help out with the family bills. They lived in a big house and had five children. In an incredibly short time she climbed to the top of the ladder and found herself in the position of vice-president of a large company. Her husband, a teacher, noticed the pressure she was under as she tried to wear four hats—as business woman, church worker, wife, and mother. Priorities of the past ceased to be applicable, as all of them, parents and children, had just become Christians and had inherited a whole new set of values.

First, the place that the family was being sacrificed was identified. That wasn't hard to do as there were no shirts ready to wear and food was never promptly on the table at mealtime. Help was hired, the children were organized to bear a reasonable load of added responsibilities, and the place of sacrifice was removed. Her husband explained the situation by saying, "I lowered *my* expectations, thereby taking away the biggest pressure of all. I stopped expecting my wife to produce on the home front at this particular time in our lives. We decided together that her business gifts needed to come first." Now this does not mean everyone has to put business or church before housework. But at that particular time, in that particular family, the unanimous decision was that mother's time must first be given to business for everyone's benefit, the kingdom's as well! At the same time nothing is cast in concrete, and it may well be that at a later date the whole situation will be reevaluated.

As a wife and mother it is hard to talk about these things with your family. For one thing, you don't want the people you love to be disappointed in you. Perhaps you've always been able to put them first, and until now the food has always been on the table on time! You think you can still do it without extra help or their added cooperation, so you try overextending yourself until you fall apart, instead of realizing that different people can carry different loads and you need knowing and understanding so that the right balance can be maintained. My friend had a marvelously mature man for a husband, who was in no way threatened by his wife's remarkable gifts and abilities, but made sure the whole family, including his wife herself, benefited rather than suffered because of them.

Pressure is good for us in many ways, but too much can be disastrous, as can too little. So keep a careful watch for the signs of strain. A caring for one another by each member of the family is certainly the thing to aim for. We need the willingness to adapt to the new phases of family living which may require a yielding of our own selfish priorities to enable another to gain a period of training experience or the freedom to work outside the home.

It is not always father who should be expected to call attention to the place of sacrifice either. It was David, Judy's older brother, who alerted me to this twelve-year-old sister's needs. Another time, I pointed out our children's problems to their father; and over the years my mother has brought many a note of caution to bear in my thinking. As our children grew older, it was my husband who encouraged me to set time aside and begin to write; and at other times I have let everything else take a back seat so I could accompany my husband on his speaking tours. We must constantly be aware of what is going on at home, trying to be flexible as changes occur. To be able to add and subtract, multiply and divide, until the sum total of "balance" is achieved at any one point in time is a challenge indeed.

First His Kingdom

Priorities are *not* rigid things. Principles are! There is the principle of making sure certain things *are* priorities—like our relationship with God, our commitment to care for each other, and a willingness to always be busy instituting reforms that will improve the lot of the family as a whole. Priorities are the outworking of those goals and will need to be "fluid" throughout our entire lives.

Jesus talked to His disciples about the matter of establishing priorities: ". . . first his kingdom . . . and all these things will be given to you as well" (Matt. 6:33). He told us that God was most important, but that "all these things"—meaning food, drink, clothing, money, and health—were certainly not unimportant, but were simply *less* important than the most important things.

"First his kingdom" is the unchanging principle for those of us who know Him, but then we have to work that out in our daily living, recognizing that the King of the kingdom will not gain much praise if, in the hectic overextension of our energies in business, church, or home, we have a nervous breakdown or our children fall into trouble because we are never around. The secret lies in basing our lives on the principle of His preeminence and working that out in our day-to-day doings. As we give time to wait upon Him, He may authorize our service by giving us peace of heart, while at other times He may instruct us to do the opposite thing and tell us so through the behavior or reaction of our loved ones.

There have been occasions in my life when the reorganization of my priorities because of my principles has meant cancellations of speaking engagements, as I have been alerted to the need to spend time serving as mother and homemaker. There have been other times when my family has canceled *their* activities so I could go and serve the cause of Christ or engage in a "business venture."

We must ask ourselves, Is the kingdom first? Is pleasing Him a top priority for me? Do I really want to do the *right* thing by Him and by His church and by my family? If we know the answer is *yes,* then we will need to work out the details in a climate of loving understanding with the rest of our family, who will hopefully also be struggling to do the same! That is what a Christian family is all about.

I have learned some practical lessons over the years as I have juggled the events of an extremely active family. I have learned to hold my own schedules lightly, like my job or Christian service or my desire for personal family time. This has helped me in the constant reorganizing of our busy doings. I have also had to learn to plan my personal Bible study at the most inconvenient times so I won't inconvenience others. I have made it a principle not to go away if everything is not set up at home before I go. When this has not been possible, I have reorganized or pulled back. I remember going through a terrible guilt trip when some help was hired for household chores so that I could get some writing assignments finished. I found peace of mind only when I came to realize that that was indeed His will for that particular period. In other words, my housework was authorized service for my house-helper and unauthorized for me! "First his kingdom" makes setting priorities not easy but possible! I believe my vocation as mother has been to live out before my children the kingdom principle—and then to help my children establish holy practices all their own.

I think of Nehemiah's marvelous example. As we read through his story, there is never a question that his top priority was "the kingdom"; but after watching him establish the principle that would dominate his entire life, we see him working it out in a variety of ways. In the opening chapters of the book, "first his kingdom" meant being the best slave he could possibly be; and then as his circumstances changed, "first his kingdom" led to some inspirational preaching and then some fancy politicking, followed by manual labor that meant staying up all night with no time to as much as change his clothes or wash himself (Neh. 4:23)! At that point his "family" must have seen very little of him, but there was no option, for God had authorized that extension of himself for the kingdom's sake.

There was a period in Nehemiah's life when "first the kingdom" meant being a soldier; and then as things eased up, it was time to regroup and set new priorities. Chapter 5 finds him with precious moments on his hands, moments that he spent with friends, entertaining strangers, and enjoying the good things of life as he kept open house. This did not mean he had lost his spiritual vision, because the whole purpose of that open home was for the kingdom. He wanted above all to be an example to his people that would help them establish a similar lifestyle. Chapters 7-13 find "first his kingdom" meaning conventions and programs and committee meetings that worked out church reforms and even some Sunday school teaching. He even managed to take time off for a trip back to King Xerxes to report all the doings in Jerusalem, because "first his kingdom" meant submission to authority, too!

Yes, Jesus knew well what He was saying when He said, "first his kingdom . . . and all these things will be given to you as well." He knew that this would be the only way we could manage time without having time managing us. "First his kingdom" means time with the King, who will authorize our days into meaningful moments, giving us a clear sense of what should and what should not be added to our schedules.

So we have learned that principles can be the basis of priorities, and priorities can be authorized by God's giving us "right" scheduling and a happy knowledge that it is indeed possible for flexible, unselfish goals to be worked out within the family structure. For this to work, enough "people time" must happen so we can be aware of the growing pains and encouragement needed for this person or that; and even the youngest member of each family must be given to understand that he or she has an important part to play within this "first his kingdom" framework.

Maybe some of you are saying, "But my family are not even believers!" Well, then, for you "first his kingdom" will mean putting all your energies into helping them to enter it! "First his kingdom" will certainly not mean antagonizing your husband by insisting on running to hundreds of Bible studies while he and the kids wait at home for their dinner! In other words, if the King of the kingdom knows that He is first in your life, He will convict you as to what needs to be "added" second, third, fourth, ad infinitum to your timetable. Spend much personal time with Him. Prayer time, incidentally, should not conflict with your duties, for God doesn't ask you for your husband's time or your children's time, but first of all for *your time.* He'll start with that and help you to go on from there.

One last practical suggestion. At the start of your week, why don't you take your calendar and write at the top of it "First his kingdom" and then fill in as a top priority your appointments with the King. Be flexible. Just because you don't have thirty minutes one day shouldn't mean He gets none! Ten will do here, five there. Keep in touch with God and ask Him to make it obvious to you just what service is authorized from heaven and what is not. He will be more than ready to help you, for He wants to be the King of your days and delights in writing eternity's busy and blessed programs into your life!

> *What is "man time" anyway? . . . God gave it,*
> *   created it for us.*
> *Dropped and suspended it in space, in the middle*
> *   of eternity,*
> *What makes it up anyhow?*
> *   Ordered moments*
> *   Packaged into minutes*
> *   Growing to an hour*
> *   Slotting into months of days*
> *   Making tidy years go by.*
> *"Eternity time" is very different from*
> *   "man time." "Eternity's time" is*
> *   "proper time."*
> *God's clocks keep proper time—*
> *   never fast, never slow, never stopping.*
> *We have to learn to live by that clock—*
> *   by God's eternal calendar!*[1]

Notes

[1]Jill Briscoe, *A Time for Giving* (Milwaukee, Wis.: Ideals Publishing Corp., 1979), p. 10.

Worksheet

A. *Discussion time*
1. What can the Valley Gate represent to us and why?
   Review these Scriptures to refresh your mind:
   a. Concerning Ahaz and Manasseh: 2 Chronicles 33:1-7.
   b. Concerning Josiah: 2 Kings 23:8-12.
2. Why do you think it is sometimes hard for us to "identify the place" where someone in our family is being sacrificed?
3. What do principles have to do with establishing priorities?
4. Do people of principle have to be rigid?
5. Read Matthew 6:25-34. How many points can you list from this passage concerning

Spiritual Principles	*Priorities for*	
	Unbelievers	*Christians*

6. How was Nehemiah an example of a man dominated by spiritual principles and priorities, yet flexible in the outworking of them?
7. Share an experience where flexibility has been exercised in your family without having to sacrifice principle.

B. *Study time: Time Management*
   Colossians 4:5 says, "Make the best possible use of your time" (Phillips).
1. Commitment of time
   Shedd says, "Our lives assume maximum worth when we turn our wills over to Him and ask that we might be of assistance to His purposes." His purposes are "in time," so it follows that He must govern our schedules if we are to be "worth" something to Him. Look up Psalms 31:15. This supposes that our committing our time into His hands is a deliberate act.
2. The redemption of time
   a. Look up and write out Ephesians 5:16 (KJV).
   b. To "redeem" means "to buy it up." How do we do this?
   c. *Our* responsibility is to give God time with us. He will then begin to manage *us*, after which we will be better equipped to manage everything else! Discuss.

    d. Example of Jesus: Look up the following verses, then discuss Christ's schedule and why it would have been easy for Him to make other things rather than His times with God a priority.

        (1) Matthew 26:36 (Who would you have wanted to be with on your last day on earth?)

        (2) Mark 1:32-35

        (3) Mark 6:46

        (4) Luke 5:15-16

        (5) Luke 6:11-12

    e. We are called to be good stewards of our time. Read Luke 12:16-21. Then answer the following questions:

        (1) What was the rich man's basic mistake concerning his understanding of time (v. 19)?

        (2) What did God call him and why (v. 20)?

C. *Quiet time*

  1. If you want to find out what your present priorities are, check your anxieties and ambitions. According to Matthew 6, this will give you a good idea of the things that are *most* important to you.

  2. Make a private, honest list of eight of your present priorities or goals in the order of their importance to you.

  3. Reorganize them as you know they *should* be.

  4. In light of what you know about yourself, is the list you have made realistic or idealistic? When you have thought about this, strike off one or two of the least important things on the list.

  5. Pray about these matters, giving God a "still" point in time to speak to you. Then answer Him!

Remember—"first His Kingdom"!

9

The Sheep Gate: Peer Pressure

Eliashib the high priest and his fellow priests went to work and rebuilt the Sheep Gate (Neh. 3:1).

As we drove past the movie theater, I noticed the title *The Last Married Couple in America*. It tempted me to sadly agree with the pollster who wrote, "Marriage is being swept into the dustbin of history." *Newsweek* magazine informs us that because of the divorce rate, one million children will find themselves with a new mommy or daddy this year. "Everybody's doing it," they say. It all seems to add up to a bad case of adult peer pressure, which brings me to the subject of this particular chapter—sheep!

If you had lived in Nehemiah's day, you would have had the opportunity to see sheep at their best and at their worst at the Sheep Gate. If you so desired, you could have stood in the shadows and watched the animals demonstrate an almost mindless necessity to "follow the leader," as they meekly obeyed their natural tendency to hurry their hooves wherever the flock flocked! Sheep are not naturally brave creatures. Just imagine the "flock shock" if one of those timid wooly bundles decided it had

had enough of being hurried along the popular path and turned around to head in the opposite direction! After a somewhat "fleet bleat," it would most surely be trampled underfoot or coerced by the crowd to conform.

No wonder the Good Shepherd depicts lost mankind as an erring flock heading off in all directions into every imaginable type of trouble. "We all, like sheep, have gone astray, each of us has turned to his own way," said Isaiah (53:6); and invariably as we go, we find ourselves pressuring the sheep around us to go along! I would have to testify to the fact that much of my teen-age mischief was not a result of conscious choice to do the things I was doing but was simply the result of following my own particular flock! It seemed so much easier to go along with the crowd than to stand my ground and say, "No!"

Everybody's Doing It

Now teen-age peer pressure is one thing, and most of us are well-aware that that is the most likely age to demonstrate a "flock" mentality—but nowdays the lambs no longer have a monopoly on the problem. Adult sheep are being pressured too. That is not to say that grown-ups have never suffered peer pressure in the past; but whereas "everybody's doing it" used to be the signal for a free-for-all between parent and child, it now appears to be the ruling philosophy among the adult population as well, particularly concerning the subject of divorce. Just as the behavior patterns of our adolescents can be socially shaped by whichever "bunch they have lunch with," so the modern marriage mind-set of the so-called mature can be similarly molded by whomever they "see for tea"!

You may ask, "But where is the pressure coming from?" I believe it is coming from a philosophy of sheer selfishness that is pervading the minds of the majority of people in our society today. It is a philosophy of an immoral majority. Then, just how are we supposed to counter this? For if we are not careful, "everybody's doing it" can give us a fatal sense of inertia. *Just who am "I" to stop doing what everybody else is doing?* we ask ourselves.

How can someone like "little ol' me" stem the flowing tide?

Anyway, since it's against our sheep natures to stand out and be different, the fact that "everybody's doing it" makes it easier for us to quiet our consciences and accept the idea that it must somehow turn out all right in the end. So we end up rationalizing our sin and calling it growing up! How can so many people be wrong? we wonder, as we look around at the intimidating crowd and decide that there is surely safety in numbers, and so it's easier to quicken our steps and gallop swiftly down the hill! "Everybody's doing it" tempts us to question old values and drastically adapt the lifestyles we have learned from the old folks, as we seek to bring things "up to date." We expect our chloroformed consciences to stay asleep long enough to let us wake us up to a changed new world where we will all feel better about our sin! "Everybody's doing it" means everybody—which could even mean me, we think secretly—and to be honest, with a certain degree of anticipation. Peer pressure, in other words, is "everybody's doing it."

Everybody Hasn't Always Done It

But let's stop a minute and think about this. Somewhere someone had to start the trend. *Everybody hasn't always done it!* Everybody wasn't doing it fifty years ago! Take divorce. Somebody got divorced fifty years ago when hardly anyone was doing it! There has to be a nonconformist somewhere, and that can give us hope. It means that trends can be slowed down and stopped in their tracks, even reversed, till everybody's doing something else! Oh, joy! Don't you see? That gives the Christian a chance to change the world! For peer pressure can surely work both ways. We can look at the whole thing negatively, or we can examine the issue positively. Sheep can be led to do wrong or they can be led to do right. Their very nature can be a bonus rather than a handicap.

Human beings have a natural desire to belong to a flock, so we can encourage ourselves with the thought—why not *His* flock? If people have sheep natures, then it should be relatively easy to influence them to follow the Good Shepherd. The first thing we need to do, then, is to begin to see the ogre of peer pressure as an angel of light. Faith and determination will go a long way to accomplish the rest!

Not long ago, a good friend of mine returned from the mission field. She was married to a pioneer missionary, and together they had served the Lord for many years in Ethiopia. As the Communist military coup took place, a coup that closed that country's doors to evangelical missions, our friends returned with their beautiful young family to the United States, where they were to await relocation orders from their board. Friends and neighbors began relating horror stories about the local "goings on" in the public schools; everywhere they turned there seemed to be a pervading and depressing sense of the almost certain doom that awaited their children, who were about to be exposed to the formidable influence of modern, degenerate America. After all, the kids had been pretty sheltered in the mission schools in Africa, Job's comforters reasoned! My friend eventually got tired of all the "woe-mongers" and declared with great emphasis, "I *refuse* to be intimidated. I believe that our children *will be the positive peers!*" I like that, don't you?

Positive Pressure

It's time we toughen up and refuse to be intimidated! Our children need to be assured that we fully expect them to be the ones to exert positive pressure on their friends; they also need to know they have positive parents behind them who have an equal determination to stand firm and reverse the trends. Example is everything. If they see us being pressured to conform to our own group and witness us sacrificing our principles to do it, we need expect nothing more from them. In other words, if our children see us keeping the rules, it will be easier for them to do the same!

"But *all* my friends stay out as late as they like. Why can't I?" wails an angry fifteen-year-old daughter. "Do you know how embarrassing it is to be the *only* one with a curfew? And why can't I go to Joe's party and have just one little drink? *Everybody* else is allowed to except me!" You can, of course, remind her that, first of all, everybody *isn't* allowed to have just one little drink, especially when they are underage and living in a state where there is a legal age-limit on drinking! Second, you can encourage her not to say she's the *only* one, but rather to say she's the *first* one! "I'll bet some of your friends wouldn't mind having a curfew," you can say cheerfully. "Rules tell you that we parents care for you, and they give you an option out of sticky situations you may not be able to foresee. Besides, you can always use it as an opportunity to tell your friends why you're different, and they'll respect you for it in the end." Talk like this will help, but only if it is followed up by a good example. Let them see you practicing what you preach!

Next, make sure you offer alternatives when you have to say no to things your children ask for. "So 'everybody's' going to Jim's after the game?" you can say to your son. "Isn't he the boy whose parents buy a quarter barrel of beer for the team? Well, why don't we give those who only go there because there is no viable alternative another option. Let's have an open house here and we'll have a pizza party for them." It is amazing what a little support, imagination, and firmness plus positive affirmation will do.

We have seen our own children move in tough secular school environments and have rejoiced as they have won their closest friends for Christ. Not only that, but they have been the means of causing many more of the flock to stop dead in their tracks, examine where their little hooves were taking them, and at least realize that *everybody isn't doing "it."* Our children's high-school years have been full of examples of the faithfulness of God, the challenge of young lives swimming against the stream, and the toughening of our precious youngsters' spiritual sinews. We have been able to remind them that any old fish can swim with the stream—even a dead one is pulled along by the current—but it surely takes a live one to swim against it! But then again we are talking of sheep, not fish, and sheep are a different kettle of fish, if you'll excuse the expression! Fish have it in them to buck the tide, while sheep don't. They need the shepherd's presence to encourage them, the rod of his correction and the prodding of his staff to remind them of their tendency to go astray, and some Christian peers around to help them stand up and be counted—and if they don't have other Christians around them, then we have to help them make some! It's as simple as that!

Choosing Your Flock

One of the ways we can help our families deal practically with their sheep nature is to talk about ways to "choose" their flock. As parents, we can start as soon as our little ones toddle off to school. Let's tell our children what sort of boys and girls we hope they will make as their friends. Let's advise them what to watch out for. Let's encourage them to look for friends among those who exhibit kind actions, have clean mouths and respectful attitudes toward their teachers. Let's tell them that there may not always be Christian peers to latch onto at first, but there will be some fine children who don't yet know the Lord (be sure to emphasize the "yet"). Let's encourage them to choose carefully, to take their time about it and not be so desperate for a friend that they make mistakes. The "group" is very important, and we should talk a lot about that with them, too. Next, let's pray about it together—starting the very first day of a new school year.

We should make sure our children see us regularly assembling ourselves together with the Lord's people. Our obvious enjoyment of a happy evening spent in the right company will not go unnoticed.

Next, we must be alert but not alarmed. It is important that fear not dominate us or else we stand a good chance of transferring our anxiety to our children, adding to their own unsureness and confusion.

I am often asked the question "Do you think there is any way we parents can choose our children's friends for them?" Well, obviously while they are small, the answer is yes. The problem comes when they are teen-agers! And yet the junior-high years provide a great opportunity to invite "the group" over to your house. In fact, you will have to invite them by the fives or tens or no one will come at all! At this age children believe the Scripture that says "two are better than one." If you happen to be teaching early adolescents, you will notice two girls will bring you a message; two boys will want to share the same job; three girls who "need" each other will complete a project together. That is why it is not realistic or even fair to expect a junior higher to do too much on his or her own. You need to plan things for the whole group and not with just the individual in mind. Barbecues, volleyball games, pool parties, and skating and slumber parties will not only give you a good hard look at your children's friends, but also go a long way toward allowing you to "choose" for them by surrounding them with the right sort of kids. This way you will have had at least a part in the forming of those close and intense friendships they will want to have at this stage of their lives.

And do remember that this is indeed just a stage. One of my favorite verses of Scripture is, "And it came to pass"; or in other words (which, incidentally, I have written in the front of my Bible), "This too will pass!" As Ecclesiastes tells us, "there is a time for everything"—a season for this and that and the other—and I believe that means a junior-high season too. Perhaps what we need to do is hang in there and know that summer will surely come!

Family Support System

I really believe that the best thing we can do for each other when we are being pressured by the flock is to stand firm and simply support each other. In other words, the family should provide the greatest peer pressure of all—a positive support system to help face the general negative onslaught from without. Let us remind ourselves of the words that can so well be applied to the family:

Two are better than one. . . .
Though one may be overpowered,
two can defend themselves.
A cord of three strands is not quickly broken (Eccl. 4:9a, 12).

Have you ever seen a plant that has grown into premature maturity? Perhaps someone has given you a bottle of plant mix filled with all sorts of artificial chemicals that have caused the plant to shoot upward with gay abandon. Its stalk is far too thin to bear the weight of the early blossoms, so it stands waving around in the breeze rather pathetically, looking as if it is about to snap. I have on occasion been guilty of overfeeding some of my house-plants in such a manner and discovered that there is only one thing to do at such a time. Find a big strong stake and stick it into the soil as close as possible to the plant. Then wait until the seedling has caught up with itself. Likewise, the greatest thing we can do for our children in their growing years is to put the great strong stick of family peer pressure next to their wavering stems and stand firmly behind them till they catch up with themselves!

A support group is what a family is all about. We can learn a lot from the excellent work going on today for alcoholics by Alcoholics Anonymous. The peer pressure afforded alcoholics there is a powerful influence in overcoming outside pressures. Half the battle is to be informed as to the group support that is available already in our churches or community.

I speak with many parents who are greatly concerned that their early adolescent children do not have healthy relationships on their own level, even though their own family is in good shape and supportive of them. I suggest to such parents: Get informed. I ask them, "What is provided for teen-agers in your church or neighborhood?" I advise them to encourage their children to join the Y.M.C.A. or some athletic programs and to find out if their church has anything vital and exciting going on for that age group. I suggest that they open their own homes after church—a place the gang can gather—and then see if they can actively lend support to any Young Life, Campus Life or other vibrant Christian parachurch youth organization operating in their area. I advise them to sign up their children for one of these weekly activities and tell them before (or while) they object that they *will* be going for six weeks. After that, if they still object, you will sit down together and discuss it. If the leaders of the group know what they are doing, I can guarantee that the youngsters will not drop out when the deadline is up.

Spend time and effort thinking of some family activities that are fun or perhaps some Christian conference that can be attended as a family, then insist on doing so even if you get some sour faces at first. Be sure to get the kids' input in these matters so they do not feel their wishes and opinions are neglected or irrelevant.

Finally, we can encourage ourselves and our children by reading some good stories about ancient or modern "sheep" who followed the Good Shepherd so closely that other mangy, hungry sheep noted how fat, happy, and satisfied they were and decided to change "flocks" and follow along, thus reversing the trends of history. We can all make such good reading available to our families. We can talk about people who started the changing process by standing alone and saying, "Though everybody's doing it, I'm not! And, what's more, everybody hasn't always done it and doesn't need to do it. If someone will come to my side, we can stand together, provide an alternate example, stem the tide of evil, and change our world!"

We need to realize that strong peer groups are usually made up of one leader and a lot of followers; and if we are not gifted leaders ourselves, we can at least look around to find the right one to support, join his or her group, and lend our weight to the Christian cause by becoming part of the changing process till *everybody's doing something else*—and God is being glorified!

Nehemiah's Example

As we close this chapter, we must return to our text. There we have a grand example of all that we have been talking about. In chapter 13 of the Book of Nehemiah we see two instances of groups pressuring others to conform and how the trends were reversed. The first instance has to do with the Sabbath day and the second with marriage. First let's read about the Sabbath.

> In those days I saw men in Judah treading winepresses on the Sabbath and bringing in grain and loading it on donkeys, together

with wine, grapes, figs and all other kinds of loads. And they were bringing all this into Jerusalem on the Sabbath. Therefore I warned them against selling food on that day (v. 15).

Now Nehemiah had been away from Jerusalem for awhile, having had reason to return to his king . . .

But while all this was going on, I was not in Jerusalem, for in the thirty-second year of Artaxerxes king of Babylon I had returned to the king (v. 6).

Coming back to Zion, he found "everybody doing it"—profaning the Sabbath day. Everybody had not been doing it when he left! In fact in 10:31 you can hear the people promising God that "when the neighboring peoples bring merchandise or grain to sell on the Sabbath, we will not buy from them on the Sabbath or on any holy day." But somewhere between that vow and the return of Nehemiah in chapter 13, someone had gone and "done it" for the first time! Someone had been the first to see an eye for a quick buck and had cashed in on his opportunity for the Sabbath-day market. It did not take long for other sheep to follow suit, and soon the trend that Nehemiah had established had been reversed, so by the time he returned, everyone was doing it! Now let's see what Nehemiah did about the situation.

Verse 17 tells us that he first "rebuked the nobles of Judah and said to them, 'What is this wicked thing you are doing—desecrating the Sabbath day?'" He said to them, *Everybody isn't doing it—I'm not!"* Then he reminded the people of the scriptural principles involved, warning them that such behavior would lead to divine judgment. Next he invited those who agreed with him to join his group and reverse the trends. He got tough about it, too, so that all could see he meant business. The very next Sabbath, he and his men stood in a conspicuous place at the gates of Jerusalem clearly demonstrating an alternate type of behavior (v. 19). This way people saw that everybody didn't have to do it! As a result, Nehemiah and his group became the trend-setters, giving others support until everybody was doing something else!

The final paragraph of this book gives us a somewhat similar example. This time the problem was "the marriage affair." Again, when Nehemiah had left Jerusalem, things had been in good shape. Listen to the people promising God to keep His laws concerning marriage:

> All these now join their brothers the nobles, and bind themselves with a curse and an oath to follow the Law of God given through Moses the servant of God and to obey carefully all the commands, regulations and decrees of the LORD our God (10:29).

They swore an oath to God saying,

> We promise not to give our daughters in marriage to the peoples around us or take their daughters for our sons (v. 30).

Yet only a few pages further on in the story we read,

> Moreover, in those days I saw men of Judah who had married women from Ashdod, Ammon and Moab. Half of their children spoke the language of Ashdod or the language of one of the other peoples, and did not know how to speak the language of Judah (13:23-24).

Once more the Jews were being pressured to conform. By the time Nehemiah returned, the problem had reached epidemic proportions!

Listen to Nehemiah as he rebuked the people: "Must we hear now that you too are doing all this terrible wickedness and are being unfaithful to our God by marrying foreign women?" (v. 27).

First, he gave the Israelites a clear call back to biblical principle. Second, he told them that wherever possible marriage relationships were to be put right. It was certainly no easy task, for the problem was all-pervasive. During his absence even one of the sons of Joiada, son of Eliashib the priest, had become son-in-law to—horror of horrors—Sanballat the Horonite, Nehemiah's greatest opponent! Right there within the heart of the congregation was a man who needed to be confronted with his wrong marriage relationship. So "I drove him away from me," says Nehemiah (v. 28). That sort of confrontation is never easy, but sometimes it has to be done if no repentance is evident and reconciliation is refused.

As far as Nehemiah was concerned, his conscience was then clear, for he had corrected what could be corrected, reiterated the rules, set guards and teachers at the gates of the city to try to prevent its happening again in the future, and then lived with the things that could not be changed. As we have this great example from the Scriptures before us, I am sure no one would accuse Nehemiah of being anything other than a positive peer. I trust no one will be able to accuse you and me of anything less!

Worksheet

A. *Everybody's doing it.*
1. Can you think of anything *everybody* is doing today that hardly anyone was doing thirty years ago?
   a. Discuss some of today's peer pressures to which *teen-agers* are subjected.
   b. Can you think of any peer pressure that *you* are experiencing at the moment? (Share, if appropriate.)
2. The Bible tells us that one of the problems with the human race is our sheeplike nature. Read the following verses: Mark 6:34; Isaiah 53:6; and Ezekiel 34:6.
   a. Divide into pairs and read Psalm 23. One of you pretend you are not yet a follower of the Good Shepherd. Using this psalm and your own words, let your partner list the reasons that you should be. (Argue a little if you like to make it interesting.)
   b. Read John 10:2 and 1 Peter 2:25.

B. *Everybody hasn't always done it!*
Nehemiah reminds the children of Israel in 13:18 that everybody hasn't always done it! The first thing *we* need to do to reverse a trend is to remind people of biblical principles. To do this we will need to know *where* to turn to in our Bibles.
1. Three of the current areas of peer pressure for our adolescents are sex, drugs, and rejection of authority.

   Look up the following verses and mark them in some way so that you can find them if needed:

	Drugs, including alcohol	*Rejection of authority*
Sex		
1 Cor. 6:15-20	Prov. 23:20-21	2 Tim. 3:1-4
	Hosea 4:11	2 Peter 2:9-10
		Jude 8

2. For the adult the main pressure to conform is in the area of *self-gratification* (1 Cor. 13:5).

   We can look at these problems under the general headings of materialism and loose moral standards.

   The following verses give some biblical principles to base our lives on:

Materialism	Loose moral standards
Hebrews 13:5	Romans 1:18, 21-32
Phil. 4:11	
1 John 2:15-17	

a. Discuss the difference between separation and isolation.
b. How many of the Ten Commandments have to do with materialism (Exod. 20)?
c. Look up 2 Corinthians 5:15.
d. Write out a summary in two or three sentences of 2 Corinthians 6:14-18.

C. *Everybody's doing something else*
To reverse trends, someone has to start by: reiterating and reminding people of principle, winning a support group, and then exercising "positive" peer pressure until everybody's doing something else!
1. What sort of things could we say to our children to encourage them to be positive peers?
Write down the three best ideas you come up with from your group.
2. What practical things could we ourselves do to be positive peers? Write down two good ideas from the group discussion that *you* can put into practice.

D. *Conclusion and prayer*
1. Look up Ezekiel 22:30 and 3:17-21. What do these verses say to you and why?
2. Pray about it.

10

The Gate of the Old: The Elderly

The Jeshanah [Old] Gate was repaired by Joiada son of Paseah and Meshullam son of Besodeiah. They laid its beams and put its doors and bolts and bars in place (Neh. 3:6).

The Gate of the Old was a valuable portal for the family at Jerusalem. If it had not been so, it would surely have been replaced instead of restored. People in our day are rediscovering the value of antiques. Age is "aped" by the craftsman on the face of brick and wood. Old is "in"—at least where inanimate objects are concerned. But what of animated age? Consider our grandfathers and grandmothers—human years dressed in human tears, grieving their "grandage."

Christians need to look at old age honestly so that we may learn to defend our extended families by becoming God's gatekeepers at this vulnerable place in the wall. Let us first consider our own old age.

Some Shocking Statistics

I remember arriving at the mature age of forty and my attention being caught by the following ditty:

> *"My glasses come in handy,*
> *My hearing aid is fine,*
> *My dentures are just dandy,*
> *But I sure do miss my mind!"*

After laughing (not too long nor too loud), I gave the little song grave thought. Acknowledging the inevitable fact that I was "getting on," as we say in England, it was good to still be able to give things grave thought—for as yet I didn't miss my mind! But what about the future? Would I miss it then? Would there come a day in my experience when I would be old and alone, destitute, or terminally ill? I can't be sure, being mercifully ignorant as to the details of my demise. But there is one thing I can be absolutely sure about, and that is the fact that I *am* terminal. This leads me to the logical conclusion that more than a mere passing thought should be given to such matters as: which of our children would find me an intolerable burden financially, or what might happen if I outlive my offspring and am forced into total dependency on strangers or a life-sustaining machine. In other words, I should most definitely consider my senior citizenship. Do I have a biblical perspective on the subject—some straight directives from God concerning my attitude toward the whole aging process in general and to my own maturity in particular?

These considerations are all the more urgent in light of the alarming reports of the terrible abuse of the elderly that are beginning to flood the media at this present time.

Walter Mondale, introducing a special report on "The Family in Trouble," tells us that even though families have been enduring institutions, they are undergoing changes, and too many are experiencing increasing stresses and pressures. One of the statistics he shares in this report is the fact that every year as many as 200,000 children are physically abused by their parents or guardians. A public affairs pamphlet by Theodore Irwin tells us that if these present trends continue, we can anticipate 50,000 deaths and 300,000 children permanently injured or disabled in the next five to ten years. This is indeed a "national disgrace," says

Irwin. And he is talking only about *physical* abuse! In recent years appalling facts concerning the battered wife have finally surfaced. And an article by Richard J. Gelles has revealed evidence from surveys conducted by professors of sociology of a new phenomonon—that of battered husbands!

"Most American violence happens in the home," Judith Gengold informs us, backing up her claim with convincing data. But it has only been very recently that "battered age" has become front-page news. In a lifestyle article, *Newsweek* unveiled a family secret, telling us that we may indeed gasp in horror at the abuse of 200,000 children. But we should save a gasp or two for one expert's estimation that between 500,000 and 1,000,000 aged parents are abused in any given year, and that number may worsen as inflation drives many more old people to move in with their families.

Geriatrics specialists are calling the physical assaults on and psychological degradation of aged parents by their own resentful children or even grandchildren "the King Lear Syndrome," after Shakespeare's aging monarch who fell afoul of his two scheming daughters! Furthermore, the problem is only marginally visible, as a battered child will be noticed by a schoolteacher and a battered wife will probably have access to a sympathetic ear or a telephone, whereas a battered parent is usually well out of sight and sound of the world, hidden away even from caring neighbors who could alert the police. Then again the old folk may refuse to complain because they are totally dependent on their children for their survival. "The ironic truth," concludes the *Newsweek* article, "is that a nursing home could well provide safer refuge for aged parents than the bosom of their own family!"

Youth Is Accountable

In light of the King Lear Syndrome, what does King Jesus say to those of us who profess allegiance to His cause? From a study of the Word of God, there is no question in my mind that we are intended to look at the whole subject of aging in a distinctly different manner than the unbeliever does. It is obvious that if people live their lives based on "time" as the ultimate reality rather than on eternity, they will view their own aging with growing horror and despair. They will fall victim to the marketers of "youth-restoring" and ointments. They will frequent health spas as time marches inexorably on, and will vainly pursue the fountain-of-youth experience through new cosmetic surgery. Some may even end up coiled painfully in crooked heaps within the white "wicker baskets" of Florida's sunshine. That is, of course, if they are wealthy enough to join such decorated age—all dressed up, but sadly with nowhere to go! The all-important element for these people is the desperate need to stay alive as long as possible.

It follows, therefore, that the presence and care of elderly parents, who may well be terminally ill and unable to care for themselves, will be a source of frustration to children who have inherited these selfish and temporal ambitions; certainly they are considered a hindrance to their total freedom to "eat, drink, and be merry." The Christian must be free of such a mind-set, knowing the Bible has both an answer to the aging process and something specific to say to the subject of the extended family. Let us start, then, by thinking about our own old age.

We are told in God's revelation that He has determined our life span, entrusting us with three-score years and ten. Psalm 90:10 tells us: "the length of our days is seventy years—or eighty, if we have the strength." The following verses of this psalm go on to remind us that since our years pass quickly and we are soon cut off and "fly away," we should "number our days aright, that we may gain a heart of wisdom" (v. 12).

Not too long ago I caught myself thinking, "When I grow up, I want to do such and such." Suddenly I realized the absurdity of such contemplations. I had grown up! Time and tide wait for no man," and I was no exception. Those birthdays of mine had kept right on coming, until they had brought me to the middle years, where I had to face the fact that I was indeed halfway through! What incentive to number the rest of my days aright, applying my heart to wisdom before it was time for me to "fly away."

With this in mind I was led to the strong conclusion that youth is accountable. Ecclesiastes 12:1 tells us to "Remember your Creator in the days of your youth, before the days of trouble come and the years approach when you will say, 'I find no pleasure in them.'" I am so thankful that I came to Christ as a teen-ager and therefore had the opportunity and privilege of applying the rest of my days to wisdom. I am grateful that I was given the chance to teach our children that *their* days are numbered also. They must remember their Creator and give Him the best of their lives. Old age *is* trouble, and we shall probably need all our failing abilities to simply "keep on keeping on" once we arrive there.

Youth is the grand season of life when the strength and energy to do and dare for God is ours for the choosing. One of my favorite verses of Scripture speaks to me of the three stages of human growth. It tells me to "wait" on the Lord, promising that if I do, I will "mount up with wings as eagles" (that reminds me of youth), "run and not be weary" (that sounds like the middle years to me), and then at the end have the promise that I shall "walk and not faint" (Isa. 40:31). For the one who makes it a lifetime habit to "wait" on Him, age is acceptable and becomes the opportunity for reflection on the faithfulness of God. It need not be a period of "dejection" about all our wasted opportunities.

Death Is Inevitable

As we "rest" our age on the Ageless One who gives sense to our years, He will delightfully prove to us that the longer we know Him, the better it will be. Yes, knowing God lends reality to youth and gives meaning to our latter days. The believer accepts the fact that life is terminal, youth is accountable, old age is trouble, and *death is inevitable*—but he is able to say with the apostle Paul, "Where, O death, is your victory? Where, O death, is your sting?" because he believes that Christ has overcome the author of death and delivered those who were all their lifetime afraid of it (1 Cor. 15:55-57). He relies on the assurance that he is not only a body, or a "tent" that is slowly being dismantled, but also an eternal being, living within that disintegrating structure, and that God is preparing an immortal heavenly home for him in Heaven (2 Cor. 5:1). He places eternal confidence in a life lived in another dimension altogether —an existence that will be forever free from the spoiling power of sin. That is why an aged believer, when asked by a well-wisher how he is feeling, may reply, "Very well, thank you, though the 'house' that I live in is in sad need of repair!"

Scripture gives us many models of godly age from the beginning of Genesis to the end of Revelation. From these, we are forced to the conclusion that old age, lent the Spirit's intelligence, knows when to open its mouth; that God paints His choicest colors in His latest sunsets; and that to know God can turn the beating years into the blessed ones! Paul exhorts older women to train the younger women to love their husbands and children and to trust God (Titus 2:4); and nowhere is this more beautifully illustrated for us than in the example of aged Elizabeth receiving and encouraging Mary, exhorting her to have faith in a God who could well be trusted to do the impossible (Luke 1:42-45).

If the youth of yesterday found it necessary for the elderly to reinforce their faith, you must never wonder if you will be needed when you are old! Elizabeth, though barren physically, was most marvelously fruitful spiritually. We are told that she and her husband walked in all the laws and commandments of the Lord—blameless; and we can pray that when we, like Elizabeth, are well stricken in years, God will send us despondent children whom we will be able to encourage by our example and by our loving acceptance of them.

Mary's world did not believe her story when she tried to tell them of Jesus, and today's youth will find the world just as hostile to their endeavors to witness to the Christ. This modern age's restive youth need the solid safety of aged faith, tried by time and tested by adversity, to give them confidence. We can take their hands and assure them we believe in God, remind them of God's ways, and be the model that they need. Above all, we will have the time to pray for them! I can honestly say I am excited about preparing myself at middle age for a ministry in my old age. God willing, I am expecting with quiet, glad anticipation the sunrise surprises of God!

Honor Your Parents

Next, let us think about our parents' old age. The Bible tells us that "religion that God our Father accepts as pure and faultless is this: to look after . . . widows in their distress" (James 1:27). If I profess to be a practicing Christian, the reality of my faith will be reflected in my attitude toward the elderly in general and to my own parents in particular. First, I am called to respect old age itself. The Word of God tells me to "Rise in the presence of the aged, show respect for the elderly and revere your God. I am the LORD" (Lev. 19:32). How long has it been since you saw a younger person rise to give his or her seat to an older one? Just as a matter of common courtesy, do our own children get to their feet when their grandparents come into the room? And when grandpa is out of earshot, are our words indicative of a spiritual obedience and a decision to indeed "Honor our father and our mother"?

I once heard the true story of a young girl who had been brought up absorbing such respectful attitudes toward the elderly. Coming to her teen-age years, she decided to "check out" her boyfriends by bringing them home—not just so her parents might approve of them, but primarily to watch how each unsuspecting beau would treat her aged grandmother who lived with them. She had no desire to commit herself to any man who exhibited disrespect for old age. On one occasion an unsuspecting date sat still in his comfortable chair as her grandmother entered the room. "On your feet, buster!", the young lady snapped crisply! It was, needless to say, their first and last evening together!

Do we "rise" to our parents—at least metaphorically speaking —honoring their age and the fact that they are our parents? Well, now, is that all there is to it? you may ask. Are you saying that all I should do is get out of my chair till the old folks get to theirs? No, that's not all there is to it at all! That's just the beginning.

The Bible tells us to portray an honoring attitude by *listening* to our parents. We are instructed to "Listen to your father, who gave you life, and do not despise your mother when she is old" (Prov. 23:22). The reasons we are told to listen to our parents are reasons that I have already touched on. Let me remind you that we are commanded to respect age for itself: and in the case of our parents, to value them simply *because* they are our parents. If we truly value them, it follows that we will value what they have to say. Whatever sort of a job we think they have or have not done as our mother and father doesn't enter into it. The Word doesn't say we are to respect our parents for the way they brought us up; it says we should respect them because in spite of what they did or didn't achieve, they gave us *life!* If it hadn't been for our parents, we would not exist at all, so at the very least we can honor them for that!

But we also need to listen to them carefully because of the wisdom they will have acquired simply because they have lived in this world a lot longer than we have and therefore must have more experience than we do! "But my parents aren't even Christians," someone objects. "How can you expect me to listen to their advice, when they don't know the Lord?" Yet, surely they have acquired experience in other areas that you can honor. *Listen where you can, learn what you can, and honor them when you can.*

Next you need to demonstrate respectful attitudes by watching your *language*. In Old Testament times, cursing your parents was punishable by death (Lev. 20:9); and Proverbs 30:17 says graphically, "The eye that mocks a father, that scorns obedience to a mother, will be pecked out by the ravens of the valley, will be eaten by the vultures." Do we allow our children to giggle and laugh at older peoples' values? Do we realize how many of our own mocking attitudes can condition our own children's thinking and behavior patterns as they listen to us discuss the in-laws in derogatory terms? Have they overheard a passing comment to the effect that it is a nuisance to have to visit the retirement home on the weekends, or what a hassle when they disrupt our routine, or what an old "skinflint" grandad has always been because he was brought up during the Depression? Do our children watch us "listening" with scarcely veiled impatience to the same old stories or anecdotes the elderly love to repeat over and over again? Or do our youngsters sense in all that is said and done by us to our parents the great sense of debt we have to repay them? For that is the attitude demanded by the Lord! Listen to Paul instructing Timothy in these very matters. Speaking of widows, he says, "Give proper recognition to those widows who are really in need. But if a widow has children or grandchildren, these should learn first of all to put their religion into practice by caring for their own family and so repaying their parents and grandparents, for this is pleasing to God" (1 Tim. 5:3-4).

Have you ever thought of paying your debts? But just what do we owe *them?* some of you ask. Let me remind you. First, we owe them for their love! We need to thank them not for parental perfection, but for loving us—always. Then we need to pay our debt for all their provisions for us. We must care financially for them because they cared financially for us! They bought us food to eat, beds to sleep in, clothes to wear, and toys to play with. They paid taxes to send us to school and gave us an education. They spent their hard-earned money so we could learn to swim or play the paino or join clubs and enjoy some of the good things this life has to offer. We have an enormous debt to repay for all that care!

"But my parents shouldn't expect that of me!" some object; or "My parents don't expect anything of me!" insist others, adding defensively, "That's what parents are for, and we expect to do the same for our children." Maybe *they* don't expect it of you, but God does!

Notice that Paul is not talking about caring for our parents when *they don't need it,* but rather he is speaking about caring for them *when they do.* He is instructing the early church to be responsible financially only for the "widows" who don't have any family left to bear the burden for them. All too often children and even grandchildren consider it the church's or the state's responsibility to look after their widows for them. For the believer this must not be so. God is pleased when *we* care, and care practically, for our own; and it follows that He is *not* pleased when we expect others to do it for us.

All this does not necessarily mean that when the time comes we do not make a place available in a nursing home for our aged relatives. Perhaps this would be the best way to care for them; and if this is so, then we would be fulfilling our responsibility to God and to them by doing so. It is really a question of our motives and attitudes. Can we honestly say before God that the course of action we are contemplating would be the best for *them;* or are we in essence saying by our actions and decisions on their behalf that this would be best for *us?* Those are hard questions to face.

You see, it is not enough to care financially for our loved ones. They deserve more from us than our pocketbooks. They need above all else to know that we consider them valuable as people and that they are still important to somebody, somewhere. Do we have a sympathetic sensitivity to their fierce desire for independence and their frustration and embarrassment of having to be dependent on us at all? Have we appreciated the fear that they may have had of becoming just so much nuisance value to us? We will have to work very hard to assure them that it is indeed a privilege and a joy for us to care and give and do, not as a mere duty, but rather as a delight. I believe that "honoring" or valuing our parents includes all of this.

The Extended Family

Now let us address the stickiest aspect of this subject. What should we as Christians be doing for the elderly who are *not* our parents? What about our in-laws, for example? And have we given any thought to the widows at church and in the community at large? To begin with, let us think about our responsibilities before God to our spouse's parents and ask ourselves if we treat them as "in-laws" or "out-laws"! Do we consider them to merely provide us with a good opportunity for a joke or two, or do we realize that they are the reason we are married? I have found that humor concerning mothers-in-law has been hilarious up to this point in time; but having reached the stage in my own experience when I am a mother-in-law myself, I am noticing a definite change of attitude when such jokes are told. In fact, recently when a neighbor told me his mother-in-law had left after a visit "on the four o'clock broom," I found myself distinctly annoyed and uncomfortable!

"Now wait a minute," some of you exclaim. *"Nobody* but *nobody* expects me to get along with my mother-in-law!" Well, I have news for you. God does! When the Lord tells us to leave our father and mother and cleave to our spouse, He does not intend for us to abandon our responsibilities toward our parents, only our dependence on them, as we transfer our allegiance to our partners. Much of the marriage conflict today has to do with the fact that people have not managed to "leave" their father and mother and have therefore not been able to "cleave" effectively to their spouse. The balance has to do with being adept at leaving and cleaving as two individuals become one new entity. I cannot say, when speaking of my husband's parents, that they are his and not mine, because we two have become one, and in the becoming, his parents have become my parents; and by the same token my parents have become his!

We must not ignore our in-laws or merely tolerate them from a distance. If we say we know Christ, we have to do better than that! I believe that all that has been stated in the previous pages in relation to my attitude to my own parents applies to my partner's parents as well. First Timothy 5 says that if any woman who is a believer has widows *in her family,* she should help them.

Nowhere in the Scriptures have we a better illustration of this than in the beautiful story of Ruth and Naomi, two women left to face a lonely and dangerous widowhood because of the death of their husbands. They chose to face it together, even though the difficulties they had as they worked out their relationship must have been overwhelming. First of all, there were cultural differences. Each woman's upbringing, education, and heritage must have appeared exceedingly strange to the other. The food they cooked, the clothes they wore, even the way they cleaned their homes, their beliefs, and their customs were poles apart, and their opposite temperaments had to complicate things. Not only this, but the confined living quarters of those times must have created many a tense situation while adjustments were being made. We are told that by the time Naomi came back to Bethlehem, she was a bitter and disillusioned woman; and I'm sure Ruth knew what it was to live with constant disapproval (a very fatiguing and discouraging occupation!).

It would have been a simple matter for Ruth to "punish" her mother-in-law by sending her off to live alone. There was nothing to stop her going her own way and making a new life for herself; but unlike her sister Orpah who kissed Naomi and went her own way, Ruth chose to cling to her instead. Deciding to identify with that bitter parent, she assured the old lady that she would go, would lodge, would die, and would even be buried with her, rather than leave her at the point of her need. In telling Naomi all those things, she shared with us the secret of such identification. "Where you go I will go . . . and there will I be buried," she said. Yes, that's what it will take if we are to truly identify with our aged parents' needs. *I* will have to be "buried"! We will need to die to our own selfishness and work at putting others first. We will have to choose a course of action that will consist of patience instead of punishment and kindness instead of criticism. We will need to learn how to give our children into our mother-in-law's arms, instead of using our little ones as weapons, knowing that to withhold them is punishment indeed!

We must be steadfastly "determined to go with her" even as Ruth with Naomi. The King James Version tells us she was "steadfastly *minded* to go with her," and I have found that in my own experience the Lord has had to help me by giving me a *"minding"* mind! I have needed to "go with her" not only at

Easter or at Christmas time, or even on her birthday, but on other days of no special significance at all. God has helped me to think of ways to touch the mundane with thoughtfulness or bring to her some small gift in my apron from "my world" that will light up her eyes. Because my mother-in-law has been included in our busy schedules, she has not been made to feel an intruder in any sense. This takes not only identification, but determination and imagination as well. Since I got married I have discovered the need to spend time thinking of all the "little" that would be much to those "new parents" of mine—the little lunch, letter, card, or phone call. We shall need to start giving them "time" rather than "things," finding common ground, spoiling them, sharing a secret or two that no one else in the world knows about—just something to show them how very special we consider them to be.

"Now stop right there," I hear you say. "You can't possibly be talking about *my* mother-in-law! You don't know her!" True! But I do know my Bible and nowhere do I read, "Honor your extended family only if they deserve it, ask for it, or expect it"! I do read, however, "Honor them anyway!" Honor them in obedience and find as Ruth found that honoring and loving, doing and giving, can change bitter women into better women. Ruth gave her only child into Naomi's arms; but perhaps she would never have done that if Naomi had not first given Boaz into Ruth's arms—for in the culture of the day, the man Ruth married was Naomi's by right. Love begets love. A mutual giving produces mutual benefits.

In that ancient relationship we read about in the Book of Ruth, the yielding of individual rights resulted in great blessing and benefit to the whole family, and so it will for us. The biblical account of this mutual submission tells us that the whole town of Bethlehem was stirred by the remarkable love story they witnessed—a love story not of a man for a woman, but of a daughter-in-law for her mother-in-law, and a mother-in-law for her daughter-in-law!

If you are a believing woman who loves the Lord and longs to let your community know about your faith, try loving your mother-in-law for a change! That will do it! The world knows little of such a commitment to one's extended family. This crazy, disintegrating society of which we are a part knows little of a love that can transcend all problems, cross all bridges, and insist on bringing the obedience of love to bear on all hard and difficult relationships. This is the love that honors God and reaps the blessings of His grand approval!

Finally, let us think about our responsibility as believers to the elderly in our church and community. The Bible tells us we are to encourage the lonely and carefully listen and attend to their needs. We must show compassion to the Christ-less and seek to lead them to Him. We are to care practically for the destitute, knowing that as we do it unto one of the least of these, we do it unto Him! When all has been said and done, we are left with an inescapable and heavy conclusion that we have a lot of hard work ahead of us!

Battered Age

Battered grannies, grandpas,
  packaged age,
    waiting patiently within the bins of
      old folks' homes,
        black cubbyholes,
          or rocking chairs—
      prisons of their patience!
Furrowed faces
  containing caked cracks
    of sagging sadness
  wrinkled wrecks of decorated decadence,
    low loose lips,
      knobbled noses,
        hoary hair,
  lapping ledges of lunch with nowhere to go,
    wedged weight
      or skinny shiny skin
        stretched tautly over
        brittle bones
      starting to snap.
Battered age
  waiting to be mailed by death
    to sweet oblivion.
We did our bit, we say.
  It costs a bundle these days to
    wrap them up so tidily.
They can't expect us to carry them
  around on our young backs
    until the postman
      comes!
How will they arrive?
  Will they get to heaven
    marked with rushed impatience,
      stamped with our indifference,

tied with knots of cold neglect,
that all our careful wrapping in
that cheap brown paper cannot hide?
And what address
upon our packaged age
we send away?
Have we made sure they know their destination?
Have we been careful to have written
heaven's home between the strings of sadness?
Have we sealed the corners of their
lives with
Scripture's certainty
of life anew?
Or are our parents simply sent away
to no-man's land?
(After all, that's where they've been
living all these years!)
Will the angels who receive them know
from whence they come?
Will they find a loving, wet, smudged,
agonized reminder on our packets
to "Return to Sender,"
knowing that's impossible,
yet telling of our
love?
Or will they arrive in heaven's depot
as if from nowhere—as if they never belonged?
Because belonging is a learned subject and
we never gave them a chance to finish
that course in the college
of our caring.
We couldn't pay the price of
schooling so expensive,
draining our resources,
tapping the treasures
laid up for ourselves.

Battered parcel,
     aged gift . . .
   soon to be given to Eternal Youth Himself
          to
     age those tired tears
       into summer smiles.
We're sorry,
   and we're so glad that there's
     still time
        STOP IT
          HONOR YOU
          AND PRAY.
We want to bring our caring
   as a timely present to
     your twilight zone of
       elongated minutes
   and your grave grey boredom.
Sharing readily—
   till you steadily respond,
We'll start with little
   so as not to startle you:
a touch—
     a strumming of our fingers on your face
       a look
          a card
            a call or
   even a visit—
Yes, even a visit–so little and yet
   so thoroughly relived
     like grandma squirrel
       hoarding winter's rations—
in case we never come again and
   spring ceases to be!
Battered age—
     let us heal your wounds
   and pour in oil and bind you up.

Forgive us—
if you can.
Touch our head—
and tell us that
you'll let us
START AGAIN
and
love you.

Worksheet

A. *Read the poem "Battered Age" to the group.*

Discuss the abuse of the elderly and comment on the possible reasons for the following statement:

> "The ironic truth may be that for all their fears a nursing home could well provide a safer refuge for aged parents than the bosom of their own family."

B. *Your own old age*

1. Are you seriously worried or fearful about any of the following and why? Discuss.

    a. Being put in a nursing home against your will

    b. The illness or death of a loved one

    c. A debilitating disease of your own

    d. Losing your looks

    e. Loneliness

    f. Rejection by your children

    g. Ending up on a life-sustaining machine

2. Fill in the following answers in your own words and then share your findings.

    a. What do the following Bible verses teach concerning the aging process?

        (1) Psalm 90:10, 12

        (2) Ecclesiastes 7:2

        (3) Psalm 139:13-16

    b. Read Ecclesiastes 11:9-12:7.

        (1) Which verses from this passage warn that youth is accountable? (Also see 1 Tim. 4:12.)

        (2) Ecclesiastes 12:2-5 gives us a poetic description of the physical deterioration age brings to all of us. Interpret it. (E.g., verse 3: "the grinders cease because they are few" is obviously talking about our teeth!)

        (3) Twice the reader is exhorted to "Remember your Creator in the days of your youth" (12:1; see also v. 6). What are the reasons given for the exhortation?

        (4) If you are no longer young, do you think it is too late to remember your Creator (Heb. 9:27)?

        (5) Share a verse from this passage that you like and explain why you like it.

(6) Share a verse you don't like and explain why you don't like it.

C. *Your parents' and in-laws' old age*

    1. What would you honestly say is your present attitude toward aging relatives?

        a. Review and discuss the following verses concerning some scriptural imperatives on the subject: Exodus 20:12; Leviticus 20:9; Proverbs 20:20; 23:22; 30:17.

        b. According to 1 Timothy 5:1-16, how many different kinds of widows are spoken about? Discuss Paul's comments concerning them.

    2. As believers, what should be our attitudes toward our in-laws and why?

Read the story of Ruth. Glean all you can from the text, asking yourself such questions as: What can I learn from this passage of Scripture? What do I need to apply to my own life? What hard thing is being said here?

        a. Ruth 1   c. Ruth 3

        b. Ruth 2   d. Ruth 4

D. *Models*

Summarize what the following people said or did that made them "models" of godly age.

        a. Samuel (1 Sam. 12:1-5)

        b. David (Ps. 37:23-26)

        c. Elizabeth (Luke 1:5-6, 39-45)

        d. Anna (Luke 2:36-39)

        e. John (Rev. 1:1; 2:9-10, 19)

E. *Conclusion*

    1. Can you share any examples of encouragement *you* have received from elderly Christians?

    2. In all honesty would you say you have accepted your own age? If not, why not?

F. *Prayer time*

    1. Spend some time in silent contemplation and prayer concerning your own old age.

    2. Share a prayer need about your parents or in-laws with a partner in the group. (Use discretion.) Pray for one another.

    3. Pray as a group about your fellowship's concern and programs (or lack of) for the elderly within and outside the church.

11

The Water Gate: Servanthood

And the temple servants [or the Nethinims] living on the hill of Ophel made repairs up to a point opposite the Water Gate toward the east and the projecting tower (Neh. 3:26).

Nethinims

These Nethinims, temple servants, whose name means "given"—who were they and why had they settled around the Water Gate? To find out, we have to go back to Joshua's day to read the story about a tribe called the Gibeonites who were "given" to Israel to be perpetual hewers of wood and drawers of water, slaves for the family of God. Joshua's mighty men had moved forward into the Promised Land, encountering many people who did not appreciate the Israelites' taking their property away from them. The kings of Jericho and Ai had tried to resist the onslaught but had been completely wiped off the map. In fact, the Bible says that "Joshua burned Ai and made it a permanent heap of ruins, a desolate place to this day" (Josh. 8:28).

As the invasion moved on west of the Jordan, the kings of that country, who had heard what had happened to Jericho and Ai, made an alliance to try and stop them. There was, however, one tribe that decided it was a hopeless cause. Recognizing that God was not on their side and that if they were to save their necks they would have to resort to subterfuge, they decided to try to make a treaty with Israel. Loading up their donkeys with worn-out sacks and old wineskins, they packed up some moldy bread, pretending they were from a distant country, and made contact with Israel's leaders. The elders of Israel "sampled their provisions but did not inquire of the LORD" (9:14), and were thus tricked into making a peace treaty with them. By the time they found out the truth, it was too late to do anything about it.

The whole assembly grumbled against their leaders, but the elders answered, "We have given them our oath by the LORD, the God of Israel, and we cannot touch them now" (9:19). They did come up with a solution, however, deciding to "let them live, but let them be woodcutters and water carriers. . . . So Joshua saved them from the Israelites, and they did not kill them. That day he made the Gibeonites woodcutters and water carriers for the community and for the altar of the LORD at the place the LORD would choose. And that is what they are to this day" (9:21, 26-27). "To this day" denotes the period of time that Israel was abiding in the will of God and was busy possessing her possessions in the land of Canaan. But between then and the time of Nehemiah, apostasy had taken place and the Nethinims, along with the people of God, had been carried away into captivity. It was somewhat ironic that the captivity set the Nethinims free—free, I would hasten to add, only to serve another master. By a strange twist of fate, it was that new master who gave them the opportunity to return to Zion. When Ezra went among the people and gave them an invitation to return with him to the Holy City, 220 of the Nethinims chose to accept his challenge.

And so having returned to Jerusalem of their own volition, we meet the temple servants in the Book of Nehemiah preparing the walls, settling down, identifying with the Jews, and submitting to their authority. Finally, we find them worshiping the Lord and promising along with the rest of the inhabitants of Jerusalem that they would not neglect the house of *their* God.

Women as Nethinims

I cannot help feeling that the story of the Nethinims may be used to depict the role of women over the centuries. In many cultures women have been "given" by men to be the hewers of wood and the drawers of water. They have had absolutely no choice in the matter. Having had no money of their own, no leisure time, and often no rights at all, they have simply been the property of their husbands to do with as they would. Thousands of them, if asked, would certainly have regarded themselves as slaves. There is obviously no time or space in this book to trace the history of women, but let me simply use a couple of illustrations.

From among the frightening army of the facts of history to do with discriminatory attitudes toward women, a prayer comes to mind. The Jewish man would pray, "I thank You, God, that I am not a Gentile, not a slave, not a woman. . . ." It must be said, however, that in the Lord Jesus' day the Jewish view of the female was vastly superior to the attitudes of many other cultures around them. The Greeks, Romans, and barbarians treated their women little better than animals. Too few of the great philosophers had raised a restraining voice on behalf of the woman's plight. True, the Roman poet Ovid had said, "If you would marry wisely, marry your equal" which must have blown out a few ancient minds as he thus challenged the men of his day with what must have been to them the totally foreign concept of equality. But sadly, such a point of view was decidedly rare.

It took a voice from heaven greeting a young teen-age girl named Mary for a new day to dawn. By the Incarnation, God forever graced womankind. "Congratulations, you are a woman," the angel said, knowing full well that women would be playing a vital role in the life of God's Son. They were to be first at His birth, last at His cross, and first to run and tell of His resurrection. Jesus always treated women with great dignity, involving them in His ministry, speaking to them courteously, and making them His friends.

The apostle Paul, who has been much maligned in this respect, actually used women in many unprecedented ways, considering the culture of his day. He trusted them as couriers of his precious epistles, a job that had previously been given only to men. There is evidence to believe that he gave women leadership in the new churches he was founding, and appreciated them as fellow laborers in his missionary endeavors. In Christ women were to be viewed as full people in their own right, equal with men in the sight of God (although this new standing did not negate the creation order of the man's authority if issues arose).

Yet women in general were still being regarded as hewers of wood and drawers of water! Even if we leave out fifteen centuries of depressing commentary and take up the story at the beginning of the sixteenth century, we find similar attitudes prevailing. History books tell us that man's accepted role during this period was that of the strong, silent, dependable protector of the one who was, without question, the weaker vessel—his wife—and whose demure, pure, pliant, obedient, and loyal role was to be assumed. She was still being "given" by the man to be his family's perpetual Nethinim!

Not long ago I saw a bumper sticker that said, "A woman's place is *anywhere she wants to be!*" This might be so in our modern day and age, but in the sixteenth century the woman's place was in the home and she was the undisputed property of her husband. And the law helped to enforce this. William Blackstone summarizes the legal status of the man in the laws of England by quoting a law covering him legally if he wanted to hit his wife. He was to be permitted to do this "as much as he chastised his servant or his child." It was not until the eighteenth century that an English law transported to the American colonies gave some relief, stating, "A rod is not now deemed necessary to teach the wife her duty. She is not to be considered as the husband's slave and the previous ancient thought to beat her with a stick, to pull her hair, choke her, spit in her face or kick her about the floor or to inflict upon her like indignity is not now acknowledged by our law!"

Elsewhere in Europe, however, things remained in pretty bad shape, reflected by the literature of the day and particularly in the proverbs that have come down to us. There is one from Spain that asks, "Mother, what is marriage?" and the answer: "My child, it is to spin, to bear children and to weep." A Russian proverb quips succinctly, "The wife isn't a jug; she won't crack if you hit her a few times!" It was Octavia Paz who said, "A woman is a domestic wild animal, lecherous and sinful from birth, who must be subdued with a stick and guided by the reigns of religion!"

But even when the law and some literature began to catch the attention of the masses, public opinion was still stacked against the woman trying to change her status. Writing of the housewife in 1908, John Galbraith said "Menial employed servants were available only to a minority of the pre-industrial population. The *'servant wife'* was available democratically to almost the entire present male population!" So there we have it in a nutshell. The wife was still to be the drudge, a Nethinim, slaving at home with apparently no choice in the matter! The sage Dr. Johnson was quoted as saying that "nature had given women so much power that the law had wisely given them very little!" Noel Coward commented, "Some women should be struck regularly like gongs."

Yet from the other side of the fence a few gifted women began at last to pen their own set of commentaries concerning their situation. "To be powerless—without social, economic or legal status, to be unconfident, dependent, insecure and vulnerable is to be female!" wrote Charlotte Bronte lucidly and bitterly. With centuries of abuse behind them and with heightened public awareness of human rights, it is therefore of little surprise to read of the birth and growth of the modern women's movement, with its roots planted firmly in the suffragettes. Women in the West simply rose to do battle on their own behalf.

And so we come to our present time and the need to recognize that there is some truth in much of what is being said today. When Patricia Cruz makes the statement that women's gifts have been ignored, she has facts and figures to back her up. She also claims that some ethnic groups have been guilty of a merciless stereotype of the female as "a docile, helpless, emotional, irrational, intelligently inferior creature who is best suited to be a sex object, domestic servant or typist!" Susan Anthony charged that women have been the great unpaid laborers of the world. "She is not paid according to the value of the work done, but according to her sex." She claims that man's argument that he is the breadwinner and therefore needs the bigger paycheck to take care of all of his responsibilities is just not true any longer.

As the divorce rate escalates, more and more women, often against their own wishes, are finding themselves to be heads of their households proving the fact that society is indeed changing in unprecedented ways. There is turmoil in the minds of many, and traditional roles are being questioned. The problem is this: just as the Nethinims of old were liberated, they found themselves serving a new master; likewise, women today who are casting off traditions of the past are also coming to the conclusion that allegiance to themselves as master is a slavery of quite another nature. Many are finding that simply getting out of the home and rid of the family is *not* the answer after all.

This is one of the main reasons I personally take issue with statements from various spokespersons for women's liberation like Mrs. Ti Grace Atkinson, former president of Now, who seeks to eliminate sex, marriage, motherhood, and love, claiming that marriage is *legalized servitude* and that marriage and family relationships are the basis for all human oppression. In the seventies, thousands happened to believe this woman and opted out of their homemaking roles. Not a few of those young and not-so-young women who testified yesterday of the liberty, peace, and joy they experienced as they walked away from their duties have since acknowledged that selfishness is indeed a most severe master. Others have made the wonderful discovery that true liberation comes from a unique freedom of the spirit as they gladly spend themselves in the service of *the* King!

In a greater or lesser degree, the choice before the women of today is the choice of the Nethinims of old. It is a matter of accepting God's concept of the family and making a commitment to the task of building the walls, hewing the wood, and drawing the water. It is a question of a glad submission to God and any authority He may place over us, recognizing it is there to protect and encourage and shelter—giving us liberty to develop all of our womanly potential.

I am not saying that a woman's only true role is to be lived out within the walls of marriage and the family, for I'm well aware of the unique position and privilege of the single woman in today's society. I am also conscious of those of you who are victims of your circumstances and are single against your wishes. For those of you who find yourselves in that situation, you can know that yours is a venerated role, for Paul tells us in 1 Corinthians 7 that singleness is to be regarded not as punishment but rather as a privilege! It can be used to serve God and His worldwide flock, for if you have no binding family involvement, you are free to go wherever He calls you. What joy to be able to attend Him without distraction! The married woman, on the other hand, will certainly suffer many frustrations as she struggles to serve her Master with divided loyalties.

But whatever role we find ourselves fulfilling within or without the structure of the Christian family, we do know one thing: that it is to be a role characterized by the "servant spirit." All Christians, after all, are called to be Nethinims, servants of their King and slaves of their God whatever their sex and wherever they live. To make good our calling and behave as such is, however, our frightening free choice. So a woman today who, figuratively speaking, is living her Christian life at the Water Gate knows that she is equal with men in the sight of God and worth dying for. Christ has set her free and she is free indeed! Because she realizes she has been saved to serve, she practices thinking servant thoughts. She knows that the apostle Peter called himself a slave of the Lord Jesus Christ and that she too needs to submit, not primarily because she is a woman but because she is first and foremost a disciple.

This idea of voluntary surrender is an exciting concept to me. I remember when I was a young Christian reading about the year of Jubilee in Exodus 21. This was the time that slaves were to be emancipated. But if a slave wanted to say, "I love my master . . . and do not want to go free," then the master could bring him to the doorpost, pierce his ear with an awl, and the slave would serve him forever (vv. 2-6). History however, does not record one single instance where this occurred! *I hope heaven does!*

Of course we cannot hope to know just what heaven records, but we do know that the Bible tells stories about men and women who were described as great servants of God. Moses was so named in Exodus 15, and in Acts 4 David is spoken of in this manner. Luke, who wrote the Book of Acts, decided to record this servant quality about King David from among many other aspects of his personality he might have chosen to write about. But then it is no small thing to be a servant. It takes all the character potential of a mighty Moses, a daring David, a princely Paul, plus a mature faith to be able to do that! So whether we are male or female, let us spend a little time thinking about this servant spirit.

The Servant Spirit

There are two main pictures of a servant given to us in the Bible. In the Old Testament Israel was called the "servant of God." In Isaiah 41:8-10, we read, "But you, O Israel, *my servant*, Jacob, whom I have chosen, . . . I took you from the ends of the earth, from its farthest corners I called you. I said, *'You are my servant'*; I have chosen you and have not rejected you. So do not fear."

In the New Testament, Christ gives us a great example of perfect servanthood. We hear about Him in Isaiah 42:1, where Jehovah speaks, saying, "Here is my servant, . . . my chosen one in whom I delight." In John's Gospel we can see this "one" fleshed out in human form, kneeling at the feet of His disciples, doing those things that only the menial slave of His day would do. On this occasion Jesus said, "No servant is greater than his master" (13:16). He also told them, "Now that I . . . have washed your feet, you also should wash one another's feet" (v. 14). We hear Him again in Matthew 20, saying, "Whoever wants to become great among you must be your servant" (v. 26).

Servants we know we should be. God has given us many examples. "But just *who* am *I* expected to serve?" you may want to know. You can't think of any disciples whose feet need washing! How can we apply this to our day and generation, to our situation, home life, and relationships? We get some help from the Pastoral Epistles at this point. Paul wrote to Timothy, instructing him to care for widows as part of his servanthood. The church is told it must look after widows who cannot care for themselves. These women must be over sixty and on a list, so that records can be kept in an orderly fashion to insure practical help and fair distribution of funds. Amidst the instructions given concerning these women, we are treated to a cameo of all those who qualify for this care. As we look at these qualifications, we can reap some information that will be meaningful to those of us who would also choose to be Christ's slaves.

First Timothy 5 instructs us to serve our children. We are to serve them by caring enough to give them perimeters—warnings and correction within boundaries that are big enough for boundless possibilities of growth. We are to serve them by helping them to come to know our God, and we are to raise them in well-managed households—which is all part of our happy stewardship for the Master.

Not only are we to serve our family in this way, we are to serve our fellow Christians too. We must be willing to do the menial tasks—washing their feet, caring for their temporal needs, etc. In other words, we must show them loving hospitality. We are not to wait for someone to ask us to entertain strangers, but rather pursue such marvelous opportunities for ourselves. And so, along with raising and ruling our children, we are to be washing the feet of the saints.

Next we are expected to help and to heal fallen humanity wherever and whenever we can. We are to relieve the afflicted, those hard-pressed by circumstances, and that means we should certainly never run out of material! We are not supposed to help fallen humanity to stand upright with our own resources, for a slave has no such things! All he is and has belongs to his Master; but because his Master has entrusted some of His treasures to him, he is permitted to spend them to help and to heal. This is where our Christian stewardship comes in. Yes, according to 1 Timothy 5, being a spiritual Nethinim will require all of our moments, all of our days, forever! So whether it be at home or at church, around us in our neighborhood or farther afield, we will never run out of people who need to be served. So when I ask myself the question, "Just *whom* do I serve?" the answer from the Bible is my family, fellow believers, and fallen humanity!

Then *how* do I serve them? The answer to that is: I serve them with a right spirit—a "gratitude attitude," not a "brat-i-tude attitude"—service with a smile. I must go about my service with a sweet spirit, conscious of the fact that I may be required by my Master to serve alone, for the servant spirit is often a solitary spirit. It is many times a silent spirit, too; and it is sometimes a still one. It is solitary in the sense of being anonymous, silent in refusing to brag about its sacrifice, still only as it waits patiently in the inner recesses of the soul, hanging in submissive readiness upon its Master's commands, willing to be guided in its actions toward the outward circumference of its personality, busying itself with the King's business!

Serving is the most marvelous vocation of all! For many years now I have sought to be a spiritual Nethinim and live out my life at the Water Gate. I am also a woman, and I'm glad about that! I have been learning to be a hewer of wood and a drawer of water since I found Christ—not because I am a woman who got married and a man bound me to himself in legalized servitude, but because I am a woman who is *first* and foremost a disciple of the Lord Jesus Christ, who set me free in my soul to sing a song of great joy, a song of spiritual service. It's a great feeling!

Make me a captive, Lord,
And then I shall be free;
Force me to render up my sword,
And I shall conqueror be.
I sink in life's alarms
When by myself I stand;
Imprison me within Thine arms,
And strong shall be my hand.

My heart is weak and poor
Until it master find;
It has no spring of action sure—
It varies with the wind.
It cannot freely move
Till Thou has wrought its chain;
Enslave it with Thy matchless love,
And deathless it shall reign.

My power is faint and low
Till I have learned to serve:
It wants the needed fire to glow,
It wants the breeze to nerve;
It cannot drive the world
Until itself be driven;
Its flag can only be unfurled
When Thou shalt breathe from heaven.

My will is not my own
Till Thou hast made it Thine:
If it would reach a monarch's throne,
It must its crown resign:
It only stands unbent
Amid the clashing strife,
When on Thy bosom it has leant,
And found in Thee its life.

George Matheson

Worksheet

A. *Review*
1. Who were the Nethinims and what does their name mean (Josh. 9:1-27)?
   a. Who carried them into captivity?
   b. How did they arrive in Jerusalem (Ezra 7:7-24; 8:17, 20)?
2. In what ways could woman's role throughout history be compared to the plight of the Nethinims?
   Do you agree we are saved to serve?
3. What clues do the following verses give you concerning true servanthood: Nehemiah 3:26; 7:46, 60, 73; 10:28-29, 39; 11:3, 21?
4. Read Philippians 2:5-8 and make a list of the different aspects of the servant attitude of the Lord Jesus Christ.
   Discuss Jesus' words: "The Son of Man did not come to be served, but to serve" (Mark 10:45).
5. The female disciple serves because she is first a disciple, which means she is a learner, a follower, and an imitator of Jesus Christ. However, like the male disciple, she needs specific instructions from her Master. Read 1 Timothy 5:9-10 and review who we female Nethinims are to serve.

B. *The Servant Spirit*
1. God is more interested in what we *are* than what we *do*. Our attitudes need to win the Father's attention and approval before our activities.
2. The servant spirit is:
   a. A *still spirit*.
      (1) Read Luke 10:38-42.
      (2) Contrast Martha and Mary.
   b. A *solitary spirit*.
      (1) Read about Elijah (1 Kings 19:9-18) and Martha (Luke 10:40). Why do you think these two servants experienced such a solitary sorrow?
      (2) How did God answer them both?
      (3) We need to remember Jesus' words in Matthew 28:20.
      (4) Do *you* find it hard to "serve alone"?
   c. A *silent spirit*.
      Comment on the following: Psalm 4:4; 23:2; Isaiah 53:7.

    d. *A supplied spirit.*
      Where shall we acquire such a constant supply of such a
      spirit (Eph. 5:18)?

3. If the following expresses the desire of your heart, sign your
name to this written statement:

Dear God, I believe You have saved me from the tyranny of
Satan to serve another King—King Jesus Himself. Thank You
for the privilege and joy of such sweet service and for the
promise of supplying Your servant spirit to my heart.

Signed _____

Your Nethinim!

C. *Conclusion*

Now go in peace and see what such a spirit will do for you and yours
as you "fight for your family"!